A Practical Guide For Raising Rabbits
And
Tanning Skins

By J. Darlene Campbell

Published by
Homeland Publishing
2014

Books by J. Darlene Campbell

The Canopus Season
The Gazebo, A Civil War Memoir
Sandalprints, Growing Spiritually

Also Writing as Darlene Campbell

The Proper Care of Rabbits
The Step By Step Book On Training Your Parakeet

Table Of Contents

Introduction
11
Rabbit Housing
15
Cage Sizes
20
Feeding
21
Beware Of Toxic Plants
29
Food From The Garden
32
Nutrition
36
Nutrition Needs For The Young Rabbit
44
Breeding
46
Colony Breeding
50
A Word About Genetics
52
Breeding For Coat And Color
57
Eye Color
61
Types of Coat
62
Kindling And Care Of The Young
64
Keeping Records
76

Diseases And Health Problems
80
Bacterial, Fungal, And Viral Diseases
82
Reproductive Problems And Genital Disease
87
Diseases Of The Eye And Ear
91
Hereditary Conditions
92
Parasites
94
Stress Related Diseases
97
Transporting
100
How To Butcher And Skin a Rabbit
104
How To Can Rabbit Meat
109
The Art Of Tanning Skins
117
Early Bark Tanning
125

Introduction

As a child growing up during WWII I remember my father keeping a small herd of rabbits in the backyard while my mother grew a Victory Garden. Rabbit was my father's preferred meat, and years later when he did not have a rabbit herd he was delighted to come home from an ethnic market bringing with him fresh rabbit meat. He never ate chicken. He had seen chickens scratching for bugs in manure piles on the farm where he grew up and said they were scavengers, so he refused to eat them. He would not even eat turkey on holidays, but rabbit was a feast.

A little research proves that rabbit meat is one of the most nutritious meats available to man, and if governments shipped rabbits abroad the world's hunger problem could be solved. Consider the advantages when one well maintained doe can produce 70 to 95 pounds of dressed, edible meat per year, and a small herd can produce enough for the grower to sell profitably. With only a 31-day gestation period a doe can raise four to six litters of six to eight fryers each in the span of one year. The young rabbits reach four to five pounds, depending on the breed, and are ready for butchering in only eight weeks of age.

When dressed out there is very little loss, 12 to 14 percent, compared to up to 50 percent loss in beef. Commercial growers use only one breeding buck for every 20 does, but the small farm grower can keep one buck for 12 does. Keeping even two does will provide

140 to 190 pounds of table meat annually for a family. This is under the best conditions. Under stress conditions where sanitation may not be the best, where stability is uncertain, there can be considerable loss in production so maintaining a few extra does is recommended for extra production, or for replacing the breeding stock.

Each year six to eight million domestic rabbits are raised in the United States for meat, fur, show, and laboratory use. Rabbit is a source of high quality meat at a fraction of the cost of raising beef. Feed conversion is excellent. Using records to verify the cost of maintaining breeding stock and raising the young, the ratio of feed to meat is 4:1, or .75 cents per pound. No other animal can be maintained in the small space allotted to a doe and produce eight to ten times it own weight in edible meat in one year. Keeping a pair of rabbits for home grown meat on the table could be the answer to survival.

Rabbit meat closely resembles the breast of chicken, is delicious, tender and all white. The nutritional value exceeds all other types of meat available on the consumer market including beef and chicken. According to the office of Home Economics, State Relations of the U.S. Department of Agriculture, rabbit is the most nutritious meat known to man. Easy to digest, low in cholesterol, and lower in calories than other meats, rabbit is ideal for today's health conscious society, convalescents, and those living under stressful conditions.

Also, rabbit manure is higher in nitrogen content than any other livestock manure, making it perfect for fertilizing the garden, fruit trees, and flowerbeds. The possibility of raising earthworms with the manure is another source of income to the grower. The worms can be raised under the cages, turning the manure into a safe organic potting soil. There are guidelines for this, so if you decide to raise earthworms it is best to visit an earthworm grower beforehand to get all the details.

If you are planning to raise enough rabbits to sell commercially, you may be interested to know that the market varies in different parts of the country with concentrated production in California, the Ozarks, Florida and the East Coast. There are 1500 known commercial growers of meat rabbits in these areas and they range from backyard growers to full time commercial operators who serve the nation's largest processing plant operated by Pel-Freeze, Inc. located in Rogers, Arkansas. You will also find processors in 14 or more states and in Canada. Animals sold for meat may be sold live to processors, so the time and work of dressing is eliminated.

While the greatest concentration of rabbit growers is in the Ozarks, many thousands more are scattered throughout the country. An independent research company estimated the total United States annual production of live weight rabbit meat to be 34.2 million pounds. Considering that the rabbit is normally marketed at a weight of four pounds, it is easy to see that nearly 8.5 million rabbits are produced in the United States each year for household consumption. If you plan to sell a few dressed rabbits rather than live, check the regulations in your area to see if a license is required.

Another source for selling rabbits is to laboratories. There is a great demand by science for rabbits, and if you are interested in capturing this market you will need a license from the USDA. Laboratories use 600,000 rabbits yearly. Since they demand a certain number of rabbits at a certain age and certain weight on a regular basis, it is easier to sell to a processor who will either sell to the laboratory or process the meat. The main biological products going to laboratories include the eyes, kidneys, and testicles. Rabbits have become so valuable to research laboratories that meat has become a by-product for the biggest processors.

As I mentioned before, I remember my dad's rabbit hutches in our backyards in California and Arizona. I watched him and my mother caring for the young, so when I moved to a farm in the Ouachita National Forest area of Oklahoma I wanted to raise rabbits. In starting our own rabbit venture, we made mistakes. There was so much more to this rabbit business than I had expected, but we learned along the way. Probably the biggest lesson learned was not to interfere unnecessarily with the doe caring for her young. It sometimes takes a litter or two for a doe to settle down to being a proper mom; so don't worry if your first litters don't make it, try again and things will smooth out. My greatest satisfaction is in toting chilled little bunnies inside my coat on a cold morning, trying to warm them while I do chores, then replacing them with their littermates in the nest box to see them wriggle and snuggle under the fur the doe has pulled for them.

Darlene

Our rabbit barn in winter

Rabbit Housing

To be successful as a rabbit grower, you must provide adequate housing for your herd. The type of housing required depends a large part on your purposes, the number of rabbits you intend to keep, and the climate in which you live. Although you will be concerned about the cost and maintenance of housing, your rabbits will be concerned about the comfort and sanitation the housing provides. What all this means is that if you live in a mild climate the herd can be caged out of doors provided there is protection from wind, rain and direct sunlight. In summer shade should be provided by trees or nearby buildings, or you can construct an overhead roof or open-end building. But if you live in a cold climate where winters are severe, then a barn or large building is necessary where you can place cages or hutches. The latter method is preferred if you are housing a large herd because the building can be heated in winter and cooled in summer. The cheapest method of heating is a wood-burning stove that heats the entire building, but lights can be suspended above nest boxes to provide warmth for the young. Try to maintain a minimum temperature of 40 degrees F. when young are kindled as the biggest hazard to the newborn is chilling.

In areas of the country where the temperatures soar well above 100 degrees F. it is necessary to find a means of cooling the herd during the summer months, because the greatest threat to adult rabbits is heat prostration. Not only will rabbits die if overheated or allowed to remain in the sun without protection, the bucks become temporarily sterile at temperatures remaining above 90 degrees F. for over 30 days. If your herd is small it would be impractical to provide air-conditioned housing, but there are other methods to keep the rabbits cool. Small blankets or towels can be soaked in cool water and placed inside the hutches for the rabbits to lay on. Another solution is to freeze gallon-size jugs of water, the type that milk or drinking water is sold in, and place them inside each hutch or cage. The rabbits will lay against the frozen jugs and cool themselves. Remove and replace the jugs when they thaw.

In the beginning, metal cages may seem an unnecessary expense, but when compared to a wood hutch the rabbits will fare far better and the expense is a much better investment. Wood hutches are satisfactory if only a few rabbits are raised, but in the long run they become unsanitary and are difficult to clean. Also, rabbits will chew the wood until you find yourself replacing part of or the entire hutch eventually. If metal cages are used, it is a good idea to provide something for the rabbits to chew because their teeth never stop growing and must be gnawed down to prevent over-growth that leads to difficulty in eating. If nothing is provided for this purpose they will chew the wood nest box, and you will eventually have to replace that as well. A small board or block of wood can be placed inside each cage to provide something for the animal to gnaw on. This chewing and gnawing is necessary too, for maintaining healthy teeth as they continue to grow, and the rabbit instinctively gnaws to prevent over-growth. The board, if large enough to rest one, also protects against sore hocks.

If you do decide on the wood route, you can build a hutch easily with 2x4s. Construct the frame about 2-foot high and no more that 2.5-foot deep. The length of the hutch depends on your chosen breed. It is recommended that 3-foot is best for small breeds, 4-foot for medium breeds, and 6-foot for large breeds such as Flemish Giants. Make the sides of small mesh chicken wire, and the floor of ½-inch by 1-inch wire mesh (do not use chicken wire). When finished, set the hutch on 2X4 legs to keep the rabbits off the ground and to protect them from dogs. It is also easier to care for the animals if they are in raised hutches.

Where space is a premium, construct two-tier hutches and place a sheet of metal between the upper and lower tiers. This metal partition should slope toward the back of the cages at such an angle as to drain urine from the upper cage to the ground, or it may be fashioned without a slope but with raised sides to act as a collector pan. The urine from the upper cage is then caught and held to prevent contact with the ground or with the cage below. These pans should be removable and cleaned at least twice a week.

Outdoor hutches with a roof for shade.

Metal cages are recommended for commercial use, but even if you house only a few rabbits, metal is preferred. They are easy to clean and are lightweight so that they can easily be suspended from the ceiling of the building with wires. Constructing these cages in units of two or three will not only save on construction costs, but will add resale value. Although more expensive, metal cages can be easily constructed from wire, and prefabricated doors and clips that are readily available from local hardware dealers or farm supply stores. For this type of cage use 1-inch by 2-inch wire mesh for the top and sides, and ½-inch by 1-inch mesh for the floor. This smaller mesh for the floor provides firm footing for your stock. Never use chicken wire for the floor as it will sag or stretch and cause injury to the rabbit's feet. A small square board placed inside each cage will act as a resting place off the wire.

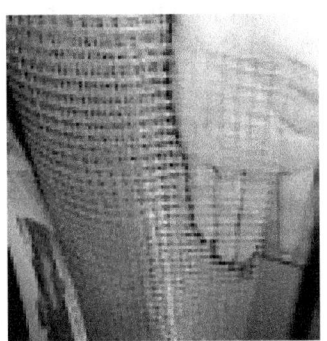

Wire mesh used for the floor of cages.
Never use chicken wire.

Cage Sizes

Like the wood hutch, the size of the metal cage is dependant on the breed being housed. Standard sizes for metal cages are as follows: Medium size breeds such as New Zealand Whites, 18 inches high and 36 inches wide by 30 inches long. Flemish Giants, 18 inches high by 36 inches wide and 60 inches, or up to 72 inches long; small breeds such as Netherland Dwarfs, 18 inches high, 24 inches wide by 24 inches long. These measurements give enough room for a nest box and for a doe to raise a litter of young.

Rabbits are clean by nature and will select one corner of the cage as a toilet, and even when the wire mesh is used for flooring the droppings do not always fall through, accumulating in this corner. Scraping this wire bottom or hosing it before it becomes heavily soiled will keep the cage clean. The build-up of hair can also pose a problem if not removed periodically. It is a good practice to keep several empty cages on hand. You can rotate the rabbits into these empty cages while cleaning the breeding cages. An extra cage or two is also beneficial when isolating recently purchased stock before introducing it to the herd, or for isolating sick animals. If you work frequently with your animals and handle them in a calm manner they will be gentle and easy to care for.

Feeding

There are different utensils and different methods of feeding. Whatever method you choose, bare in mind that nutrition is of utmost importance so select utensils by the feed you intend to use such as hay or pellets. When a few animals are kept, rabbits may be fed and watered from crocks if feeding pellets. The crocks come in different shapes so choose the ones that best fit your needs. Those with rounded, sloping top and sides make it more difficult for the young to climb into and soil. When the young bunnies reach the age of eating solid food, they will climb into the crocks to sample what is inside. Before changing to another method of feeding, we used slope sided crocks for feed and straight-side crocks for water. The case against crocks is that they take up floor space within the cage, and in cold climates where the water can freeze, the crocks frequently crack.

Feeders and water bottles that attach to the outside of the cage are easily filled and they do not use needed space within the cage. Outside feeders should have a mesh or screen bottom to allow dust from the pellets to filter through. Also, feeders attached to the outside will remain cleaner as young rabbits will climb into crocks to sample adult feed and will soil it, but are less likely to climb into a metal feeder attached to the outside of the cage.

There are two main types of rabbit water bottles; Flip-Top and Screw-Bottom. Flip Top bottles will save you time due to the fact that you don't have to take them off the cage to refill. Flip Top bottles however tend to be more expensive than the typical screw bottom rabbit water bottle. Using water bottles instead of bowls will generally save you maintenance time and keep your rabbits' water supply cleaner.

The most important element in maintaining a healthy herd is water. No animal can survive without this necessary element. Several factors affect the amount of water a rabbit will consume; one is the temperature of the surrounding air. Rabbits are extremely heat sensitive animals and will consume great quantities of water during the warm months. This water disperses heat and helps adjust the animal's body temperature.

Water also helps to remove impurities from the body, aids in digesting food, and functions in moving nutrients to and from the cells of the body tissues. It constitutes up to 75 percent of the adult animal body, and as much as 95 percent of the weight of the newborn. A 10-pound rabbit will drink about 2/3 quart of water a day. This amount may increase during lactation or with warm weather. Due to the importance water plays in nutrition and health it must be kept before the rabbit at all times.

There is no need for automatic watering systems unless you are considering a commercial venture. In this case, freezing may be a problem in winter, but the pipes can be wrapped with heat cables, or heat cables can be inserted inside the pipes and thermostatically controlled.

In our own herd, rabbits are watered from crocks. These work satisfactorily as long as the temperature remains above freezing. When winter temperatures take a dive and the water in the crock freezes, it is almost impossible to get the water to thaw without damage to the crock. Frequently, the freezing alone will cause cracking and leakage, so we never fill the crocks completely full during severe weather. By taking a tea kettle or bucket of hot water to the rabbit barn each morning when setting out to do chores, a little warm water is poured into each crock to hasten the melting of ice. During severe weather the herd needs to be checked and water offered several times a day if the crocks are frozen.

Simple water bottles that attach to the outside of the cage are well and good in warm climates or in heated barns or for summertime use. For commercial use there are more elaborate water bottles or systems that are heated and thermostatically controlled in winter.

Salt is another important element in feeding. However, pellet feed contains necessary salt along with other important minerals. Adding salt in the form of a salt spool is common and the rabbit probably enjoys it, but it is not necessary. Salt aids in getting the rabbit to drink more water during warm weather. Not offering salt is not going to affect the health of the herd as rabbits naturally obtain the necessary amount from feed.

It is far easier, safer, and cheaper to feed a commercially made product that meets all nutritional requirements than to understand the subject of nutrition when attempting to meet your herd's dietary requirements. Improper feeding leads to disease, rickets, anemia, low fertility and poor growth. On the other hand, with good feeding, good management and disease control a herd can be maintained in fit condition for top production. There are different types of pellets available on the market. If you cannot find a commercial rabbit pellet in your area all-alfalfa turkey crumbles can be substituted as long as you supplement with grain.

Even though supplements are not necessary when feeding a good quality commercial feed you may want to add quality legume or grass hay to the diet occasionally. Legumes are alfalfa, lespedeza, cowpea, vetch, peanut, and clover have a protein content that is four to five times higher than that of good grass hay. Protein is vital for growth, maintenance and reproduction. Some does, due to lack of protein, will develop cannibalism. Although killing and eating the young can occur from fright it is more often due to poor nutrition.

Commercial rabbit pellets contain all
the nutrients necessary for healthy

Many commercial breeders and fanciers who show their stock add a protein supplement to the feed schedule as a matter of routine. We feed Calf Manna to pregnant does. A teaspoon or two of this pellet supplement started a few days before kindling and continued for the first week after kindling helps to curb cannibalism and aids in lactation. In place of Calf Manna a high protein meal may be used such a soybean, peanut, sesame or linseed. These are excellent supplements, but must not be mixed with whole grain since much of the meal will settle to the bottom and be wasted. If whole grains are fed, supply the protein in flake, cake, or pellet form.

High quality hay can be used as a daily ration when supplemented with grain. It will provide a source of protein and balance the grain ration. Choose legume hays such as alfalfa, clover, lespedeza, cowpea, vetch or peanut. Grass hays such as timothy, prairie, Johnson grass, Sudan grass and carpet grass are less desirable because they are less palatable hays and contain about half as much protein as legume hay.

For easier feeding, chop coarse hay into 3 or 4-inch lengths to reduce the amount of waste. Leafy, fine-stemmed, well-cured hay can be fed whole.

Rabbits also enjoy grain. Grain is a very basic part of the diet and is already added to most pellet feeds. When offering grain as an occasional treat or supplement, oats, wheat, barley, sorghum grain, buckwheat, rye and soft varieties of corn may be fed. Other treats rabbits enjoy and that will add additional vitamins, minerals and proteins come from your own garden such as root crops like beets, carrots and turnips or fresh greens, rapidly growing grasses, cereal grains and palatable weeds that are free of pesticides. Be careful when feeding fresh greens as over-doing it can cause loose stools. Root crops can be an excellent supplement in the winter when fresh greens are not available.

There are three methods of feeding rabbits and each method has its advantages.

Free Feeding: When feed is kept in front of each rabbit at all times it is known as free feeding. This method is used mainly when growing young rabbits to table size, when conditioning an animal for show, or when feeding pregnant and lactating does. Each of these situations is considered a stress condition.

Limit Feeding: Limiting the amount fed to each animal is limit feeding. This method is used to prevent over consumption of feed which leads to overweight. An overweight rabbit is less likely to reproduce. Bucks that are not in service and dry does are fed by this method. It is also used after weaning a litter to aid the doe in stopping the flow of milk.

Hand Feeding: This is daily feeding the amount the rabbit would consume if feed were kept before it at all times. Enough feed must be fed to maintain a steady rate of growth in young animals and to keep mature members of the herd in top condition without excess fat. This is a preferred method in most rabbitries when it is combined with limit feeding. It is ideal for does in production and for growing young.

A little known fact is that rabbits re-ingest their food. It is normal for the rabbit to re-ingest a soft matter passed through the digestive track. By excreting two kinds of feces, one hard and one soft, the ingestion of the soft provides a source of B vitamins. This vitamin is synthesized in the cecum by bacteria that are present. The cecum, a part of the intestine, normally synthesizes all the B vitamins the rabbit requires. The rabbit also needs certain amounts of vitamins A, D, E, and K in addition to crude fat and fiber.

When considering a source to purchase your rabbit's hay or pellets, avoid purchasing from grocery stores and pet store chains, as the feed may have sat on the shelves or in a storage warehouse for months, which makes it stale and lacking in proper nutrient values. Vitamins lose potency over time; so purchase good quality pellets and hays from local feed stores that are in the business of providing quality feeds for farm animals. Some rabbit veterinarians also sell high quality pellets, but at a higher price than local feed stores.

If you desire to feed a daily variety of fresh vegetables due to an abundance of such feed from the garden, feed two to four cups of fresh vegetables for each five pounds of optimum body weight. All vegetables should be fresh, washed and organic whenever possible. Pesticides sprayed on vegetable tops can be deathly to rabbits.

Offering fruit should be limited to no more than one or two tablespoons of high fiber fruits (pears, apples, tomatoes...) per five pounds of optimum body weight, one or two times a week; not on a daily basis. Fruits are high in sugar and can cause obesity which leads to infertility.

Feeding your rabbits a limited amount of high fiber pellets, abundant fresh grass hays and a daily assortment of fresh vegetables is a key factor in keeping them healthy. Take all changes to the diet slowly. Quick changes can cause diarrhea or an overgrowth of bad bacteria in the gut. Also keep in mind that different rabbits have different dietary needs. Younger rabbits, elderly rabbits, smaller breeds such as the Netherland dwarf, large breeds like the Flemish giant and long haired rabbits all have different needs, and you should consult your rabbit vet for more specific information.

A rabbit that is free to roam the yard is exposed to toxic plants.

Beware of Toxic Plants

While providing a varied diet for your stock may seem beneficial it is not necessary. Commercially prepared rabbit pellets contain all the needed nutrients your rabbits require for good growth and reproduction.

Perhaps the rabbits themselves enjoy a change, so if you are inclined to add fresh greens to your animals' diet be careful not to include toxic plants. The damage done by these poisonous plants may not be immediately apparent, but over time they can range from diarrhea to death. The following is a list of plants that you might find in your garden, pasture or woodlot, along with a few familiar houseplants. Avoid these at all costs.

Also avoid feeding grass clippings that have lain in piles and soured. It causes colic.

African evergreen
Amaryllis
Azalea
Belladonna
Blue-green algae
Boston ivy
Calla: calla lily
Castor bean or castor oil plant
Chinaberry
Chinese evergreen
Chives
Dumb cane
Elephant ear
Foxglove
Garlic
Hemlock
Holly
Hyacinth
Iris
Jimson weed
Kalmia
Laburnum
Lords and ladies (cuckoo spit)

Marijuana
Mushrooms
Narcissus (Daffodil)
Nightshade
Onion
Peace lily
Philodendron
Pieris (fetterbushes)
Poinsettia
Pathos
Predatory bean
Purple thorn apple
Rhododendron
Rhubarb
Shamrock
Spindleberry
Spoon flower
Tobacco
Tropical cyclades
Tulip
Virginia creeper
Wild calla
Wisteria
Wooly pod milkweed
Yew

Black Magpie rabbit at show

Food From The Garden

While you may occasionally feed your rabbit a bit of fruit, it is extremely important that you limit their intake to no more than one or two tablespoons of high fiber fruits (pears, apples, tomatoes...) per five pounds of optimum body weight, one or two times a week. Optimum body weight is how much your rabbit should weigh according to the breed standard, not its present weight.

Feeding the required amount of high fiber pellets and abundant fresh grass hays is the key factor in maintaining a healthy herd. Keep water available at all times. If feeding from the garden, take all dietary changes slowly. Quick changes to the diet can cause diarrhea or an overgrowth of bad bacteria in the gut. Also, different rabbits have different dietary needs. Younger rabbits, elderly rabbits, smaller breeds such as the Netherland dwarf, large breeds like the Flemish giant and long haired rabbits all have different needs and consulting with a someone who specializes in your breed can prevent problems before the start.

VEGETABLES (AND FRUITS) THAT ARE GOOD FOR RABBITS

VEGETABLES	FRUIT
NOTE: When feeding from the garden at least three different vegetables a day are recommended - any combination of lettuces counts as ONE veggie for that day)	*NOTE: Limit feed only once or twice a week in small amounts - **NO seeds or pits!** Sugary fruits, such as bananas and grapes should be fed only as occasional treats, and NO fruit should be fed to rabbits that are overweight.*
Alfalfa, Radish And Clover Sprouts Asparagus Basil Beet Greens Bok Choy Broccoli	Apple Blackberries Blueberry Pineapple

Brussels Sprouts	Melon
Carrots And Tops	Papaya
Chard	Peach
Chicory Greens	Plum
Cilantro	Pears
Clover	Raspberries
Collard Greens	Strawberries
Dandelion Greens	
(Pesticide Free!)	
Eggplant	
Endive	
Escarole	
Grass - Freshly Cut From	
Your Backyard,	
If You Are Sure There Are	
No Chemicals, Fertilizers,	
Poisons (Park Grass	
Usually Has One Or All Of	
These)	
Kale	
Mint	
Mustard Greens	
Mustard Spinach[3]	
Okra Leaves	
Parsley	
Pea Pods (A.K.A. Chinese	
Pea Pods)	
Peppermint Leaves	
Peppers (green, red,	
yellow...)	
Pumpkin Leaves	
Radicchio	
Radish Tops	
Raspberry Leaves	

Squash: Zucchini, Yellow, Butternut, Pumpkin Turnip Greens Various Lettuces, Avoid Very Light Hearts: Romaine, Butter, Green Leaf, Boston, Bibb, Arugula... No Iceberg Watercress Wheat Grass	

NO LEGUMES OR NUTS! These are not natural foods for rabbits and they can be very dangerous to gut function.

On our farm we never offer fruit of any kind, but do offer on occasion greens from the garden. Fruit will mold and ferment if not eaten immediately, so be sure to remove any uneaten remains.

Nutrition

Although there are more than 50 identified nutrients a rabbit needs, only a few are critical enough to pay attention to, because the rest are plentiful in a normal rabbit diet. If you feed commercial rabbit pellets, the feed company has taken the worry out of supplying your rabbit's dietary needs. Basic requirements include:

Protein:
The rock-bottom *minimum* protein requirement for rabbit survival is approximately 8% protein. Feeding rabbits at least 12- to 14% protein is ideal for adult bucks and does with no litters. Lactating does should receive at least 17- to 18% of their diet in protein.

Commercial pellets meet the rabbit diet protein needs with alfalfa and soybean meal, among other forages. If you can only find pellets with 16% protein and want to provide your rabbit with less protein, simply feed fewer pellets and increase the grass hay portion of the diet.

Carbohydrates:
Readily digestible starches and soluble fiber, and relatively indigestible, such as cellulose. Carbohydrates are for energy, and some can actually boost immune system function (beta-glucans). But carbohydrate overload can cause an explosion of bacteria in the gut, and if this includes toxin-producing bacteria, the rabbit can die quickly of enteritis. Carbs are important, but they need to be balanced with fiber.

Fats:
Fat is digested in the small intestine. Fat levels as high as 25% in the diet have had no ill effects on the rabbit. Normally however, you can expect a 2-5% fat level in pelleted feeds. Show rabbit breeders may add a little oil by top-dressing in order to enhance rabbit coat condition.

Minerals:
Calcium is easily absorbed by the rabbit, and any excess is excreted in the urine, leaving behind white deposits in and below their cages. Mixing legumes and alfalfa offers a balanced supply of calcium and phosphorus. Pelleted feeds also include mineral additives: Magnesium, sodium, potassium, chlorine, sulfur, iron, copper, cobalt, manganese, zinc, iodine and selenium. Deficiency diseases for most of these minerals is unknown.

A note about cobalt: The only known nutritional role for cobalt is to make up a part of vitamin B12 (cobalamin). Additionally, no specific nutritional requirement has been identified.

Coprophagy is the act of consuming feces. The practice of coprophagy in rabbits ensures that they consume a large excess of B12. You may have seen rabbits doing this--they bend themselves around and nibble at their hind end. This is an important nutritional behavior for rabbits - they're not usually cleaning, they're eating their 'vitamins,' so to speak

A *cecotrope* is the technical term for the soft clusters of feces that come straight from the cecum. They look a bit like grape or raspberry clusters, are surrounded by a thin membrane, and are rich in vitamins and bacterial protein. Cecotropes provide the rabbit with important nutrients and vitamins that have been synthesized by gut bacteria, including Vitamin K and a plethora of B vitamins, including Vitamin B12. Scientists have put collars on rabbits so they could not eat their stool, and their nutritional status quickly declined.

Rabbits do not eat the hard round 'marbles' you find beneath the cage, only the soft clusters. And the rabbit only consumes it directly from the hind end. If a cecotrope should fall to the ground, the rabbit will not eat it.

To better explain how this works lets look at the rabbit digestion system. As with all mammals, digestion begins in the mouth. The food is mashed up by the teeth and mixed with saliva, which contains proteins that begin breaking down the food. When the food is swallowed it enters the stomach where it is mixed with stomach acid and digestive enzymes, which continue the digestion process. It then moves out of the stomach into the small intestine where nutrients are absorbed into the body, and then it continues on into the large intestine where the food particles are sorted by size. The larger particles of indigestible fiber drive the smaller fragments of digestible fiber *backwards* into the cecum, which is a large blind-ended sac located at the junction of the small and large intestines. The indigestible particles are then passed out in the fecal pellets, and the cecum begins the fermentation process that will produce what is commonly referred to as night feces or cecotropes, which a rabbit will ingest directly from the anus. You can tell the difference between normal feces and cecotropes by their soft, shiny clumped texture and often more pungent odor.

A rabbit's cecum maintains a delicate mix of protozoa, yeast and *good bacteria*, which is crucial to keeping your rabbits healthy. If something upsets the delicate bacterial balance, such as stress; the over-use of antibiotics, a diet too high in fat or too low in fiber; too many carbohydrates, *bad bacteria* will begin to grow. These bad bacteria produce toxins that can be harmful or fatal to rabbits. On the other hand, the products of *good* cecal fermentation are crucial to healthy gut flora, because through coprophagy, the oral re-ingestion of the cecal pellets produced by this fermentation process, the rabbit can absorb by normal digestion the special nutrients and vitamins contained in the cecal pellets. Some evidence suggests that bacteria from the cecal pellets help the food digest while it is still in the stomach.

Pellets and Hay: Hay provides a prime source of fiber, which is instrumental in keeping the gut in good working order. Rabbits with higher protein needs such as older, sick, angora breeds and show rabbits are fed alfalfa hay rather than grass hays as it is higher in essential nutrients such as calcium and protein. Feeding commercial pellets ensures the rabbit will receive all necessary minerals in correct balance and also provide the necessary fiber for a healthy gut. It is far better to feed a complete pellet than to try meeting all your rabbits' needs with homegrown feeds. Garden cuttings should be considered a supplement and not a main diet.

When considering which pellets are preferable for our herd consider that young rabbits under one year old can free-feed as much as they want a fresh, plain, high fiber (18-20%), mid-range protein (14% - 16%) pellet. Adult rabbits should get 1/4 cup of low protein (10% or lower), high fiber pellets PER DAY per five pounds optimum body weight. Optimum body weight is the desired weight for the breed, not the current body weight. Do not feed commercial pellet mixes that contain seeds, dried fruit or colored cereals. These commercial *treat* foods are geared to look pleasing to humans, but they are definitely not in the best health interests of your herd. By nature, rabbits are not seed, fruit or cereal eaters and these types of *foods* are high in sugars and carbohydrates, and can lead to an overgrowth of bad bacteria, as well as becoming overweight which leads to infertility.

When rabbits are fed an improper diet, that is, one that does not contain an adequate amount of fiber or one that is too high in carbohydrates, the gastro-intestinal tract cannot function properly and it begins to shut down, causing various degrees of what is called GI stasis.

What is GI stasis? It is the slowing down or stoppage of the contents within the gut. When the speed with which material moves through the gut is altered it can affect how quickly the stomach and cecum empty. When this happens we often see a dramatic decrease in the rabbit's appetite for both food and water, which only furthers the problem: The body still needs water to function so it takes it from the stomach and cecum, causing the contents of the entire GI tract (food, hair from grooming, etc.) to become further dehydrated and impacted. The rabbit is then unable to pass the mass of food/hair in the stomach, feels full, uncomfortable and often gassy due to the build-up of the bad bacteria in the cecum. At this point the rabbit will often stop eating, become anorexic and die. When a rabbit dies from GI stasis and its related problems it is most often due to the toxins produced by the bad bacteria in the cecum.

In most cases, especially those caught early by the observant grower, GI stasis can be reversed with time, *patience* and good advice from a qualified rabbit vet. Your goal is to prevent it from happening at all.

Salt: If for some reason you feed minimal or no pellets, in other words, if you attempt to raise all the feed for your rabbits on your farm and keep to feeding farm raised grasses and vegetables, you will need to find a way to add salt to the rabbit's diet. Most rabbit growers haven't used salt spools in years, however if necessary, you can hang a mineralized salt spool in the rabbit's cage.

The mineralized salt spools usually contain:

- o Salt
- o Zinc
- o Iron
- o Manganese
- o Copper
- o Iodine
- o Cobalt

Vitamins: Dietary vitamin requirements are quite low in rabbits. Fat-soluble vitamins A, D, and E are usually supplemented in dry pellets, as are Thiamin (B1), Riboflavin (B2) and cobalamin (B12). Because of coprophagy the rabbits' vitamin and mineral needs are fairly low. This runs their food through a second time, so they can absorb a second helping of nutrients

Age, moisture and light destroy vitamins in feed! Providing old feed can dangerously mess with your rabbits' nutrition. After a few months, commercial pellets lose their nutritional optimum. Pellets older than 3 months old in most cases are unlikely to keep your rabbits healthy. Keep feeding it, and your rabbits will lose their conditioning due to vitamin loss, not to mention fertility. The animal may also go off its feed and get diarrhea, possibly due to some budding mold growth in old feed.

Feeding rabbits extra vitamins is not necessary if feeding a balanced pelleted feed. We do an extra high protein supplement spiked with vitamins and minerals, to our pregnant and lactating does during gestation and the first 2 weeks of lactation in the form of Calf Manna. One tablespoon a day is top dressed on the pellets.

Water: Water is the most essential ingredient in rabbit nutrition. A rabbit can go many days without feed, but only 3 or so days without water.

Ideally your rabbit should have access to an unlimited source of fresh water every day. This can be provided by an automatic watering system, bottles that attach to the outside of the cage, or by containers that rest on the floor of the cage such as crocks or bowls.

Winter can prove a challenge due to frozen water tubing, valves, nozzles and crocks. In wintertime when our water freezes, we carry fresh water to our rabbits morning and night, and sometimes noon as well.

If winter lasts for many long months in your area, you might consider warmers for your watering system tubing.

Black Silver Fox Doe

Nutritional Needs For The Young Rabbit

Baby rabbits grow at a tremendous rate, therefore the nutritional needs change rapidly from birth through the first couple of weeks of nursing. This is reflected by the composition of the doe's milk. As an example, the colostrum (first milk of the doe) will have a high fat content (greater than 17%) and by the fourth day it drops to around 10% but steadily increases to over 15% by the eighteenth day. However, after the third week it begins to taper off to less than 13% fat.

It is interesting to note that the lactose (carbohydrate) content of rabbit milk only varies between 1.1% and 1.7%. This means that baby rabbits obtain energy from fat and not from carbohydrates although a small amount is important.

The diet of the lactating doe will influence the composition of her milk as well as the amount of milk she can produce. Does on a high fat diet will increase milk production that leads to increased health of their young.

By the third and fourth weeks baby rabbits are beginning to consume appreciable amounts of solid food. At this early age you will find them in the doe's feed bin as they sample the pellets or available hay. Most rabbit foods have low fat and high carbohydrate contents that can make the switch from the doe's milk difficult. In fact baby rabbits have been shown to fair better on high fat diets. Trading calories from carbohydrates for calories from fat leads to a more efficient use of protein and energy.

Since our young weaning rabbits begin sampling feed from the doe's bin at an early age, we do not change their diet at weaning time, but continue feeding the same diet as the doe was previously fed. They make the change gradually on their own since they are still nursing the mother while sampling her feed. When the weaning is complete, we feed the young straight pelleted feed, although there are products on the market available if you are weaning young for show or prefer faster growth and weight gain.

Depending on specific needs for feeding rabbits, there are several different formulas of pellet feed available. Check with your feed dealer on differences that include: 18% protein for rabbits requiring higher nutritional levels of protein, 16% protein for the commercial breeder and show competitor, 15% protein suitable for all rabbits, and a specially formulated pellet when animals are under stress such as being shown. All pellet types are considered nutritionally complete so there is no need for feeding a salt spool.

A Californian doe in good condition with bright eyes, well fleshed and dark markings.

Breeding

It is important to know how to sex a rabbit so you do not put animals of the same sex together or they will fight. Also, you need to know how to sex the young weaning age rabbits. To do this, cradle the rabbit in your arms, and using your forefinger and middle finger press down on the rabbit's vent area which is just in front of the anus. If the rabbit is a buck the penis should protrude. If the rabbit is a doe you should see a slit or central line running up and down.

The age at which time breeding begins depends largely on the breed and the individual rate of development of your breeding stock since different breeds mature sexually at different ages. Preferably, bucks of the smaller breeds should not be used for service until five months of age. Bucks of medium breeds should not be used for service before the age of six months, and the large breeds should not be used before nine or ten months. At those recommended ages they may service one doe a week until fully mature. A mature buck can satisfactorily service one doe a day, or preferably every two days and remain in condition. When a buck is used too heavily he will lose weight and become unthrifty.

The doe should also be at least six months of age although small breeds may mature as early as four or five months while giant breeds may delay maturing until eight or ten months with males maturing later than females. Watch for signs of heat to determine when to place the doe with the buck. The doe is always taken to the buck's hutch and the mating should occur almost immediately. When the mating is completed return the doe to her own cage.

Some signs of heat are restlessness and nervousness. The doe will rub her chin on the feeding and watering containers, or may attempt to join other rabbits in nearby cages. Since rabbits have no regular heat cycle they can be bred almost any time. The doe will ovulate six to eight hours after the first mating with the buck. Since ovulation occurs only after a mating has taken place you may wish to allow several matings to insure adequate stimulation for the release of eggs. Remove the doe as soon as one or two matings have taken place to prevent fighting. There are differences of opinions on breeding, so what works well for you should be the method that you use. Although this one breeding is usually sufficient, some people will breed one time and remove the doe for six or eight hours then rebreed.

You may want to test the doe to see if she has conceived and one method to determine if she is pregnant is to place her back in the buck's cage two weeks after breeding her. Usually a pregnant doe will become aggressive and refuse service from the buck, and if she isn't pregnant she can be rebred at this time. But this is not always an accurate method since some does will accept service when pregnant, and others will refuse service when not pregnant.

The only accurate method to determine pregnancy is quick and easy, and can be learned with a little practice. It's called palpating. Palpating is done between the 12th and 14th days after mating. To palpate, place the doe on a flat firm surface. Hold the ears and the skin over the shoulders in your right hand and place your left hand slightly in front of the pelvis between the hind legs. Now use your thumb and fingers of the left hand to gently apply pressure to the abdomen. Move your fingers and thumb backward and forward. Handle the doe gently, using only the slightest pressure. If she is pregnant you should be able to feel the embryos as small hard forms as they slip between your thumb and fingers. If you are unsure of the diagnosis the doe can be palpated again a week later.

Occasionally a doe will not breed when introduced to a buck. She may be fearful if this is her first mating, or she may simply have an aggressive nature. In the latter instance, she can be restrained by the handler until the mating is completed.

A doe that is a show rabbit should not produce more than two or three litters a year if you want her to stay in condition for showing. Arrange the breeding of show animals to allow the litter to be weaned before showing.

If the doe is not a show rabbit and she is raising young for meat and fur production, she can be bred throughout the year as long as adequate housing is provided. If a litter is lost at the time of kindling, she can be rebred as soon as you feel it is advisable.

A nursing doe can be rebred when the litter is six weeks of age. By this method a healthy, productive doe can produce four litters a year and raise them to the weaning age of eight weeks.

Since one buck can service ten does satisfactorily, it is not necessary to keep many bucks. If the buck is mature and healthy he can be used several times a day for short periods of time. In this way, the young that he produces will be close in age and at weaning time it is easily determined which of the young should be kept or sold. When the young are spaced several weeks apart it is difficult to select the better rabbits since age can make a big difference in their size and development. It also allows the handler to determine which of the does are producing the better young.

A doe that has been maintained in condition can produce litters until she is 2 ½ to 3 years of age.

Colony Breeding

A very simple method of breeding is called the colony method, and is ideal when raising only a few rabbits for your own use because it eliminates the need for expensive caging. Where rainfall is frequent or heavy, entire litters of newborns will drown at the first downpour and the burrows will collapse. Older rabbits escape flooding conditions by seeking high ground within the compound, but newborns are helpless. A variation of this method is to move bred does to cages before they kindle, although you will not know the date they were bred.

Space permitting, a colony consists of one buck and several does maintained on the ground of an enclosed area. The walls or fence must extend two feet below the surface of the ground to prevent the rabbits from escaping, which they will do when the herd becomes large or over-populated. The does will dig into the earth to kindle, and pull hair to make a nest. These underground burrows keep the rabbits cool in summer and warm in winter. But as mentioned earlier, in a heavy rain the burrows will collapse and all young rabbits will be lost.

If you do not remove the doe to a cage at the time she is due to kindle, and she delivers her litter underground, you will not know the litter size nor the exact age of the young. That is why it is preferable to move her to a cage with a nest box when the litter is due.

If you are colony breeding and have roughly eight does in a pen on the ground, remove each doe and palpate every ten days. Those that palpate positive are moved to individual cages and are given a nest box two days before the expected day of kindling as the exact date of breeding is not known. In most instances the doe will rebreed the same day she is placed back in the colony after weaning her litter, so a calendar can be kept with dates as to when to palpate, etc. Never place more than one mature buck in a colony as they will fight.

New Zealand White Littermates

A Word About Genetics

Although you don't have to be an expert when it comes to genetics, every breeder needs to know the basic laws governing inheritance in order to avoid the pitfalls of half-hazard breeding. In order to set a type in which all the off-spring will be uniform in coat, color, size, markings, production and constitution, or in order to improve on any of these, a breeding program must be established. When breeding unrelated animals it is more or less like playing roulette. You spin the wheel and what the resulting offspring develop into is purely a guess or chance.

In establishing any breeding program it is always best to start with breeding stock that possess those characteristics for which you are aiming. These characteristics are passed on to the next generation. There are three breeding methods that need to be understood and those are in-breeding, line-breeding, and out-crossing. It is essential that the rabbit breeder understands the basics of each method.

In-Breeding: This is the system most used to achieve results quickly because it will decrease the amount of variation between individuals and make them more alike in genetic makeup. It also is used to set a type once a strain has been developed through several generations of breeding. In an in-breeding program closely related individuals are bred together. That is father-daughter, mother-son, and brother-sister. One must be careful in selecting breeders because in-breeding will increase the chance of faults appearing in the off-spring if those faults have been carried in the line as recessive genes.

Line-Breeding: Here, more distantly related animals are bred together. The pair to be mated will have some ancestor in common. This is where pedigrees are important. A pedigree will list all ancestors back as far as the researcher wants to go, or as far back as the breeder has maintained records. When one is familiar with the ancestors and their desirable characteristics it is easy to set a type or continue a trait with this method. This is the mating of cousins, aunts with nephews, or uncles with nieces.

Out-Crossing: This system is the mating of completely unrelated individuals within the same breed. It will increase the amount of variation within a litter as you are adding to the gene pool instead of doubling on like genes. Out-cross mating may add a hybrid type vigor, but will not aid a breeder in developing a breeding program.   Too many disappointments occur here because when a recessive gene appears it is not sure which parent carried the recessive. Recessives can be carried undetected for several generations then pop-up unexplainably. Such bad traits include buckteeth, splay legs, shallow chests, etc.   Out-crossing has its advantages when selecting an outstanding type from a known strain with no known recessive faults.

The rabbit breeder needs to establish a program that will produce the desired results. For example, do you want rabbits mainly for the table? Then you will look for rapid growth, steady weight gain, and a well-developed meaty carcass.

Are you raising rabbits primarily to sell to laboratories? Then select for breeding those individuals that conform to the specific requirements of the buying laboratory. Usually that is a specific weight at a specific age.

Are you raising rabbits primarily for the fur industry? Then you will look for prime coat and color pattern. Usually the buyer of fur desires a solid white coat that can be easily dyed to any color. However, they may want a specific color pattern so that dying is unnecessary. You will breed for a lush thick pelt.

Are you raising rabbits for show? Then you will need to know the standard for the breed you are raising and will select individuals for breeding that have the desired size, shape, and coat pattern to pass on to future generations.

When looking at your first litters and deciding which to keep for breeding and which to sell or keep for the table you will be looking at traits that are evident to the eye. Depending on your purpose for raising rabbits look for traits that will achieve that purpose.

The best method to begin any breeding program is to purchase stock from a reputable breeder who keeps accurate records and pedigrees. Most important is the buck. Since the buck will be bred to many females and will produce many more young than the doe, he must be able to pass on to the young his finer qualities. The ability to do this is called *prepotent*. Bucks that are not *prepotent* pass on the genes inherited from ancestors, but which may or may not be the finer qualities. The offspring do not live up to expectations. Animals that have been line-bred for several generations will almost always be *prepotent* and will pass their finer points no matter what doe they are bred to.

The doe is also important. If she carries poor quality, even though the young show the good qualities of the sire the doe's faults could turn up in the next generation or so.

When introducing a new bloodline to your herd the first offspring, generation one, will carry 50 percent of each parent's bloodline. Say that you have purchased a new doe and breed her to one of your bucks. That first litter will be 50 percent of the new line you introduced. Mate these young animals to animals in your herd that are related to the your buck, generation two, and the young will possess 75 percent of your bloodline and 25 percent of the new bloodline of the doe that you purchased. On the next breeding, that is the next generation, those offspring can be bred to different animals still related to the sire and this will give you offspring with 7/8 of your old blood, and 1/8 of the newly introduced blood. Through this type of breeding you will have introduced new blood without sacrificing the fine characteristics within your own line.

A Giant Chinchilla Buck
Photo courtesy of Dr. Hagen Graebner

Breeding For Coat And Color

The decision to produce the perfect color and the perfect coat draws many rabbit raisers into the mystery of genetics. It is a challenge that inspires the fancier to show his/her animals in an attempt to win ribbons as proof of excellence.

When striving for specific colors the breeder is working with genes that control the coat color as it is visible to the eye. There are at least ten known series of genes that act and interact with each other to produce the colors of every known breed of rabbit, and these genes are not visible. Only by breeding do the colors show themselves to our liking or to our dismay.

Genes are either dominant or recessive. The dominant gene in any series is always listed with a capitol letter, and the recessive gene or genes are listed by a lower case letter. If there are more than two genes in the series to produce a certain color, then letters can be added to differentiate between the genes. They are always listed in the order of dominance with the dominant genes at the top of the list and the most recessive genes at the bottom.

Surprises occur because some dominant genes will blend with the recessive genes on the series to produce an intermediate effect, while some dominant genes will completely dominate and hide the recessive genes that are present.

Every living thing carries only two of the genes from any given series but will pass on only one of them through the sperm or egg. The young, then, will receive two genes; one from each parent. Littermates will each receive different genes from either parent, thereby showing different colors.

For example, if the buck is Aa (agouti color, but carrying a recessive self-color gene), he can pass on either the dominant *A* for his agouti color, or the recessive *a* to the young. Some of the litter will receive the *A*, and some will receive the *a* gene. If the doe is also carrying the *Aa* combination, she will pass on only one or the other to each of the young in the litter. Some will get the *A*, and some will get the *a*. The litter could have a mixture of *Aa*, *AA*, or *aa*. This is where your recessives come into play and show themselves as unexpected colors, by receiving the two recessives *aa*. Even so, perhaps none of the young receive the *aa*, but still carry one *a* to pass on to future generations until paired with another recessive *a*, when it shows itself.

There are many coat colors and patterns seen among the different breeds. The most prevalent being the white rabbit with pink eyes. This is found in many breeds and is indicative to albinism as there is found no pigment anywhere on the rabbit.

There are also Blue-Eyed Whites that are found in breeds such as the Netherland Dwarf. This is pure white with only the eyes having a blue pigment. This color pattern is also known as Vienna White.

Then there are patterns known for colored points, where certain areas of the fur are colored such as the nose, ears, feet and tail. Colored points are seen in the Himalayan, Jersey Wooly, Holland Lop and Netherland Dwarf.
The Californian is a Pointed White and it is found in several breeds such as the Rex and Mini Rex. Another Pointed White is the Dwarf Hotot. This breed is solid white with a narrow band of black around the eye. The eye color is dark brown. This unusual marking makes the rabbit very attractive.

Aside from white rabbits there is a large assortment of color patterns found among the different breeds. These patterns are divided into three groups.

Agouti: This coloration shows three bands of color on the hair shaft. The colors alternate from dark to light, to dark.

Tan: Similar to the Agouti pattern is the tan pattern. It is basically the same as in the Agouti, but the hair shaft is solid colored without bands.

Self Pattern: This pattern shows itself in a solid color rabbit with no other color present.

Blue Eyed Netherland Dwarf

Eye Color

It is the coat color genes that also control eye color, and rabbits can have brown, blue, red/pink, or gray eyes. The eye colors are determined by the coat-color genes and never vary. That is to say that all densely colored rabbits will always have brown eyes, dilute-color rabbits will always have gray eyes, albino whites and pointed whites will always have pink eyes, and Vienna Whites will always have blue eyes.

Types of Coat

There are four different coat types among the various breeds of rabbits. They are basically the normal coat, the satin coat, the angora coat, and the rex coat.

The normal coat is what is seen in the majority of breeds. It is produced by dominant genes and is dominant to all other coat types. There are two types of this coat, one that will quickly fly back into place when stroked from rump to head, and one that will slowly fall into place when stroked from rump to head.

The Angora coat was probably one of the first mutations to occur among rabbits. Because of its length it lends itself to spinning and the making of garments. The Angora coat is found on the English and the French Angoras, the Giant Angora, the American Fuzzy Lop, and the Jersey Wooly. The body color may appear lighter than the face, feet, and tail due to the longer length of body fur. Because it is a recessive gene, it must be bred only to other long coated or angora rabbits to maintain the luxurious length and color.

The Satin Angora coat is finer than the regular Angora wool. It has a luxuriously rich color due to the smaller, thinner hair shaft, which is also transparent. This coat is due to recessive genes.

The Satin coat is a recent mutation showing up in 1930. It is easily identified by the satin sheen. This is another result of recessive genes.

The Rex coat is an unusual and interesting coat type. It is plush and velvety and is the result of a mutation occurring in the 1920s. It is very short and plush like velvet. The softness is due to the outer guard hairs being the approximate length as the under coat. To retain this coat, Rex coated rabbits should only be bred to another Rex coated animal due to it being recessive.

English Angora

Kindling And Care Of The Young

The doe's gestation period is 31-32 days. A nest box is usually placed in the doe's cage a day or two before she is due to kindle with a little nesting material placed on the bottom. If the box is placed in the cage too early she may use it for a toilet. The nesting material of straw, dry grass of cedar shavings is layered on the bottom of the box to a depth of at least four inches, and preferably six or eight inches if grass or straw is used since the doe instinctively tunnels to the bottom and the material will settle. The doe will investigate the box and rearrange the material to her liking.

Nest boxes are necessary for several reasons; not only does it keep the young off the wire bottom of the cage and confined for easy care, but it protects the young from harm. Many a newborn rabbit have lost one or more legs when a stray dog discovered it dangling helplessly through wire netting.

The exact size of the nest box depends upon the size of the breed you are raising. The box should be large enough for the doe to make her nest, but small enough to discourage her form remaining in the nest once her motherly duties are performed.

Recommended sizes for nest boxes are as follows

Small breeds such as Netherland Dwarf: 12"x8"x8"
Medium breeds such as American White: 15"x10"x10"
Large breeds such as Flemish Giant: 18"x12"x12"

Nest boxes are easily constructed from plywood. There should be three tall sides, and one low side. This low side should be low enough to enable the doe to enter and exit without injury to the udder by bruising, yet high enough to prevent the young from rolling or toppling out. We find four to five inches works best on this low side for our New Zealand Whites and Californians.

When housed in a building, the box should not have a cover as moisture may accumulate on the surface and drop back down onto the young rabbits. However, when the cage is exposed to the elements a top is preferred but it should be removable to provide easy access for inspection of the litter.

On the day of kindling the doe will be restless. She may dig frantically at the bottom of the nest box and will pull fur from her body to line the nest. Occasionally a doe will wait until after she kindles then quickly pull large amounts of fur to cover the newborns. Most litters are born at night without complications.

If the doe does not pull fur and the litter arrives on the bare floor of the box, or as sometimes happens when a doe is bred for the first time, on the wire of the hutch, you must pull fur from her sides or throat and cover the newborns yourself. She will know what to do on her next litter.

Young rabbits cannot maintain their body temperature and the mother's fur has high insulation qualities to keep them warm. The doe will quickly learn what to do and will enter the nest to care for her young. Be aware that should one or more of the young rabbits happen to fall out of the box the doe is helpless to pick it up and return it to the nest. She will nurse only those young remaining in the nest, or those which have fallen out of it, but not both groups. If you find young and helpless babies on the wire, pick them up gently and place them in the nest box with the rest of the litter.

The average litter size is seven or eight young. It is natural for the mother to spend much of her time out of the nest, entering it only long enough to nurse and then leaving again.

Part of the work involved in raising rabbits is the checking of litters each morning. Any young which have fallen from the nest box or which may have been dragged out by the doe should be picked up and placed with the rest of the litter. Any young that feel cool to the touch should be removed and warmed inside your shirt or jacket so that it receives your body heat as you

Heat lamps suspended above breeding
cages supply heat during cold weather.

go about the chores in the barn. When it begins to move
and feels warm to the touch it can be placed with its
littermates, making sure that it continues to receive heat
from those around it. Young rabbits have a jump reflex
and will automatically jump upwards to attach
themselves to a nipple when the doe enters the nest box.

Most does do not object when the litter is inspected
daily if done in a quiet, calm manner. But if the doe
appears nervous or aggressive then some tempting treat
can be offered to keep her occupied while the young are
examined. The baby rabbits are born hairless with a
healthy pink color and with eyes and ears sealed.

After the doe has kindled and left the nest the litter
should be inspected. Remove any dead, deformed or
undersized young. When the litter is too many for the
doe, surplus young can be moved to the nest of another
doe whose litter is the same age. To do this we use a

very small amount of Campho-Phenique rubbed on each of the baby rabbits, the ones being added to the nest box and the ones belonging to the foster doe. This way all the young smell the same and the doe will accept the new arrivals as her own.

The greatest hazard to newborns is chilling. His thermostat is not yet working and for this reason the fur the doe pulls to cover the young has remarkable insulating qualities. Because the young are warm at birth, she covers them to retain that warmth. If one or two of the young become chilled they can seldom be saved. Chilling occurs when the doe kindles outside the nest box or when temperatures inside the rabbit house drop dangerously low.

There are several methods to revive young rabbits that have become chilled. The one we practice has already been mentioned, placing a young rabbit inside your shirt. Another method is with an electric heating pad or electric blanket. Be careful not to overheat, as it is just as dangerous as chilling. The temperature of the blanket or pad must be at the lowest setting. The chilled rabbit is placed on the pad that has been covered with a towel so the young rabbit is not in direct contact with it, and covered lightly with a cloth until it is revived and ready to be returned to the litter box. Do not leave the chilled rabbit on the pad any longer than it takes to revive it, as the pad can over-heat, leading to death. Even when you feel the pad is not hot, it can be too warm for the young rabbit if left indefinitely. If you must leave it on the heating pad for any length of time then place a folded towel between it and the pad. If no electricity is available, warm a blanket on the wood stove and line a small box with it. Then place the chilled rabbit on the warm blanket and place the entire box and contents behind the wood stove to keep warm. Turn the bunny over from time to time to warm both sides equally, and as the blanket cools replace it with another warm one. Towels also work well.

Wood frames support metal cages inside the barn.

Corrugated metal awnings provide shade as well as deflecting wind and rain. The barn is constructed with open sides of chicken wire on the upper half for ventilation. In winter this section is covered with heavy plastic to retain heat.

Rabbit house/barn under construction.

The completed barn.

A well-equipped rabbit house, especially one that is a commercial venture, will have heat lamps over the nest boxes or heating units within the boxes. This ensures warm quarters even though outdoor temperatures drop below freezing.

When the does are kindling in hot weather there is the problem of keeping the young cool. Young rabbits move away from each other in the nest when they are too warm. If they spread out some may not find the doe at nursing time. Remove some of the fur covering them or in extreme heat as experienced in the southwest it is all right to remove all the covering.

The young rabbits begin to leave the nest at 19 or 20 days of age. They should be fat little fellows showing that the doe is a good milk producer. If the young begin leaving the nest at a younger age it is a sign that they may not be getting sufficient milk from the mother, or the temperature within the nest may be too warm.

By the time the babies are eight weeks old, they are eating well on their own and are removed from the doe's cage. At this time they can be weighed and the future breeders are selected from the rapid growers, while the slower, underweight individuals are culled. The ideal is to produce litters in which all the young are close in weight.

Sometimes the food a doe eats will go to fatten her instead of producing milk for the young, so her young will grow more slowly. This is why records are kept, to record the better producers and to cull the also-rans. A good rule of thumb is to wean at eight weeks of age, as by this time the young are eating well on their own, and a supplement feed can be added if necessary.

The author places weanlings in a separate cage from the mother and feeds them for two weeks before selling them or putting them in the freezer. This allows them to gain an extra pound. Prospective breeders can be selected at that young age. Look for good confirmation, strong bone, dense coat, and if breeding for fur or color, nice markings. It is best to know the qualities desired for your particular breed, so talking with other rabbit breeders and obtaining information from breed clubs as well as attending rabbit shows will teach you what to look for in your breed.

When evaluating your young rabbits hold each one in your hand and feel the body. The rump should be round and full. If this trait is not evident at weaning time, it never will be. The youngster should have a good wide loin to balance and support the well-filled rump. There should also be a good spread to the ribs. This rib spread allows for ample lung room, and as the lungs develop, so will the chest and the shoulders. A good flat, broad chest will almost always develop a good set of shoulders. If the young rabbit has a narrow, sharp breast it will never improve.

While you are holding the young rabbit, place two or three fingers between the front legs and compare several of the young in this manner. It is easy to feel which of the litter have a sharp, narrow chest capacity and which have ample capacity for lung development.

As for the head, fur, or ears, it will depend on the particular breed you are raising. It is sometimes difficult to access the fur in the young weaning age rabbit, as it still has a soft, immature coat. It will take several months before the full adult coat replaces the juvenile coat. Only by attending rabbit shows and viewing other rabbits of the same age and breed will the novice breeder get a good idea of the type to breed for and the type to cull.

The weaned litter is now ready to be recorded separately from the doe. Each rabbit that is kept is given a number and will have its own record, either on a hutch card or in a record book. Even if you are a hobby breeder, you should strive to become an authority on your breed, and keeping accurate records allows you to follow the accomplishments of your herd.

Those prospective breeders should be placed in their separate cages at no later than 12 weeks of age to prevent them from breeding too early.

Many does lose their first litter from lack of experience. Remember that time brings its rewards, so breed the doe again. If a doe cannot raise a litter after three tries, cull her. If the doe does not conceive at the first breeding it is often due to being over-weight. This happens frequently with a mature doe that is allowed to rest between litters. She collects excess fat around the female reproductive organs, which can prevent conception. Always cut back on a doe's feed to stop her milk supply, and then keep her on maintenance rations only if you do not intend to breed again right away.

Hutch cards are numbered to maintain basic records of the rabbit in each hutch, and the information is transferred to a record book.

Keeping Records

Every successful business or project is dependent on maintaining accurate records. We depend on records of one sort or another for every aspect of our life. The bank sends us a monthly statement as a record of our check cashing transactions and our pharmacist keeps a record on every prescription we have filled. Our mechanic will even keep a record of when the car last had a tune-up. So it is when raising rabbits. We maintain records of when animals are bred or born, shown or sold.

With rabbits, record keeping becomes an exciting experience because it shows the day-to-day goings on of the herd. It can be as complicated as you make it revealing such facts as sales of breeding stock, meat sold, furs sold, equipment purchased, feed costs and so on. Or it can be a simple breeding record of which doe is bred to which buck and when the does are due to kindle.

If you keep financial records, and you will if you become a big operation, you must set up a book to maintain every expense you incur and every item that you sell. You will list the purchase of feed, equipment, medication, advertising and gasoline if you transport. You must keep receipts and enter these into the record system for tax purposes.

Breeding records should be maintained on each rabbit you are breeding or intending to sell as a breeder. These records are kept on hutch cards, which are later transferred to a book that contains additional information such as pedigree. Hutch cards are easily made of index cards and attached to the sides of hutches to give reference to breeding, or you can purchase them as well as pedigree forms through the American Rabbit Breeders Association.

However, such cards are quickly soiled and look bad, so by using a filing card system it eliminates the soiled cards. This filing card system is set up by making an index card for each breeding rabbit, and placing the card in a small filing box. Every hutch has a number permanently attached to it that coincides with a number on a card in the file. In our rabbit barn we have metal cages resting on wood frames, and the numbers are painted on the frames with black paint. Each rabbit is assigned a hutch number, and the card is a record for that particular animal. Rabbit supply houses sell glass-faced cardholders to protect the cards if they are attached to each hutch, but it runs into an additional expense, so I find it less complicated to make up a filing card for each numbered cage and keep it in an index box in the barn. That information is later transferred to a record book. All the information found on the card is transferred to a book that is kept along with other record books such as those used for tax purposes.

On the front of each hutch card enter information as to breeding date, date kindled, number of young born, number of young raised to weaning age, weight of weaned litter. Also include the number or name of the buck to which the doe was bred. Maintain this same information (omitting date kindled and number of young raised to weaning age) for each buck. This will soon tell you if a buck is producing fast growing heavy weight offspring and to which does he is better paired.

On the back of the card enter notes on such things that are pertinent to you such as "aggressive", "shy", "good mother", "foster mother", "breeds readily", "conceives consistently", "good nurser", "builds good nest", "lost last litter", or dates of such things as illness and medication administered, or date purchased and from whom. When you are building up a herd nothing in the rabbitry should be left to memory.

The best method of correctly identifying each rabbit is the use of tattoos. This method involves having every rabbit tattooed in the left ear and then making a numbered card corresponding with the tattoo. The reason it is important to identify your animals is because many breeds are identical in looks, that is to say they have the same size and markings, yet each one carries a different set of genes. It is the genes that produce the desired results when breeding for selected traits in a herd. If two identical rabbits with different bloodlines become mixed up, you could possibly introduce some faults or recessive genes to the herd, and then hoping to rid the herd of those traits, sell the wrong doe when she becomes suspect. Read more about genes in the chapter on breeding.

Tattoos are permanent identification and you can tattoo your own rabbits by purchasing the equipment. Using a combination of letters and numbers you make up your own ID for each rabbit. Animals that are to be shown must be tattooed in order to compete. Only the left ear is used for this purpose as the right ear is reserved for registering the number of a champion. If you are unsure about the tattoo procedure it is best to consult a rabbit veterinarian and have him/her do the first tattoo. Then you will be more comfortable with it and can tattoo the rest of your breeding stock yourself.

Champion Dutch Rabbit

Diseases And Health Problems

Even if you keep your rabbits healthy through sanitation and good management, eventually even the best-managed herd will develop some health problems. Most of us recognize simple ailments such as diarrhea or abscesses and can treat them with remedies we use on other animals on the farm. There are some diseases however, that are peculiar to rabbits alone, such as sore hocks, which can prove troublesome unless you know what the symptoms are.

The best remedy for disease is prevention, and often prevention means isolation. This is not to imply that rabbits are to be kept in isolated quarters, but that visitors should be kept to a minimum. Persons can carry disease from one rabbitry to another, so it is best to avoid showing your stock to strangers who may have spent the day visiting various herds, or who may have sick rabbits at home.

Stray dogs, cats and wild animals such as mice, rats and wild rabbits also are carriers of disease and contaminants. Store all feed in covered containers so as to prevent the invasion of mice, and never introduce a new rabbit to the herd without knowing about the health of the herd it comes from.

Just like humans and other animals, the infectious agents that cause disease in rabbits are bacteria, viruses, parasites, and fungi. Although direct contact is necessary in some instances it is not always necessary as viruses and fungi are carried in the air. This explains how an outbreak of a virus can spread rapidly through a herd.

Learn to give antibiotic shots yourself; you will save a lot of veterinary expense in the long run. Listed here are the most common rabbit ailments along with their usual symptoms and treatments to make rabbit raising what it should be —uncomplicated.

Bacterial, Fungal and Viral Diseases

Abscesses

Symptoms: Lumps under the skin in the back, neck, cheek, or dewlap areas.

Cause: Abscesses are a collection of pus caused by the invasion of a bacteria, streptococcus.

Treatment: Clip the fur from around the lump. Using rubbing alcohol or iodine, sterilize the area. Make an incision in the lower portion of the lump and squeeze out the infective material. Clean the incision with peroxide and apply an antibiotic ointment. Thereafter, apply antibiotic ointment twice daily or use a topical spray or powder such a Furazolidone.

Fungus Infections

Symptoms: Patches where hair is missing with a flaky, dry crust. The lesions appear on the nose, feet, around the mouth, on the eyelids and on the backs of the ears.

Cause: A fungus invasion of the hair follicles. Fungus is transmitted by persons handling the stock, or spread from one rabbit to another on contact. This condition is also transmissible to man so caution should be used when handling infected animals.

Treatment: Rub a fungus powder or ointment into affected area daily until new hair growth appears. Replace bedding in nest boxes and apply fungus powder to the fresh bedding to prevent transmission to the young.

Metritis
Symptoms: A white, thick putrid discharge 7 to 10 days after breeding has taken place. This infection can invade the uteri and cause sterility in the doe.

Treatment: The infection is difficult to reach and it is recommended that affected does be culled from the herd as they may cause bucks to develop orchitis.

Mucoid Enteritis
Symptoms: Diarrhea as evidenced by feces on the hind feet or not forming into the usual round pill shape, hunched back, rough coat, grinding the teeth, or sitting hunched over the water dish with front feet in the water. The stomach may be bloated and the eyes appear to be squinting.

Cause: Fifty percent of all rabbit deaths from birth to 8 weeks of age are caused by mucoid enteritis. The exact cause is not known, but it is suspected to be caused by one or more of the following; coccidiosis, intestinal parasites, fungi, virus, unsanitary conditions and/or improper feeding.

Treatment: A water-soluble antibiotic, terramycin, aureomycin, or neoterrmycin can be added to the drinking water at the rate of 1 teaspoon per 2 ½ gallons of water. Continue treatment for one week. As a preventive measure, the entire herd may be treated with a low level mixture at the rate of 1 teaspoon per 5 gallons of water.

Sulfaquinoxoline or sulfa solutions such as Sulmet which are primarily used by poultry breeders prove to be highly beneficial when coccidiosis is the cause. The amount recommended for poultry is printed on the label of the bottle and is satisfactory for rabbits. Mix this solution with the drinking water and offer as the only water available to sick animals, or use it periodically to treat the entire herd as a preventive measure.

Since the death rate is high with mucoid enteritis, it is recommended that all animals that die be disposed of by burning or burying. Do not administer two drugs at the same time.

Myxomatosis
Symptoms: Inflammation and swelling of the eyes, ears, nose and genitals accompanied with high fever. The death rate among mature animals is high.

Cause: This is a virus infection affecting rabbits only along the west coast of the United States, Mexico, and South America. It is spread by biting insects such as mosquitoes.

Treatment: The best control is prevention since there is no cure. Spray or drain mosquito-breeding places. There is a vaccine proven to be effective in the prevention of Myxomatosis.

Pneumonia
Symptoms: Rapid breathing, a temperature above 103 degrees, nasal discharge and a bluish tint to the eye color of albinos.

Cause: Drafty, cold or damp quarters. Stress and a general run down condition that weakens the rabbit's ability to fight off bacterial infections. The infection invades the lungs and nasal passages. It is a major killer of adult rabbits and can infect and kill a rabbit within 24 hours. Suspect pneumonia when a member of the herd is discovered dead without any previous sign of illness.

Treatment: Speed in diagnosing and treating this disease is utmost important. Inject penicillin deep into the hind leg muscle following the dosage recommended for rabbits by the manufacturer. Penicillin is a good antibiotic to keep on hand by the rabbit breeder to fight a variety of illnesses and infections. Continue the recommended dosage for 2 days past the last sign of symptoms.

Snuffles

Symptoms: Snuffles is called by many breeders the common cold in rabbits because of the nasal discharge. There may be sneezing prior to the runny nose. The affected rabbit tries to wipe away the discharge with his front paws.

Cause: An infection entering the mucus membranes of the nasal passages due to stress and lowered resistance.

Treatment: Treat the entire herd by administering a water-soluble antibiotic such as aureomycin in the drinking water. Follow the manufacturer's directions on the package, usually 1 teaspoon to every 5 gallons of water. Do not use metal water containers while using this medication.

Penicillin may be given by injection. Do not use two medications at the same time.

Sore Hocks

Symptoms: Sitting in a hunched position. Inactivity and off feed. The presence of scabs or sores on front or hind leg hocks. Infection may cause swelling and inflammation.

Cause: This is a painful condition that is caused mainly from unsanitary conditions in the cage, sharp wire flooring, or cage bottoms that are not solid enough to support the rabbit's weight without sagging. Some rabbits inherit thin fur covering on the feet and are more susceptible.

Treatment: Wash the sores with mild soap and water. Apply an antibiotic ointment until the condition clears, or administer ¼ cc of injectable penicillin daily. Placing a board on the wire cage floor will give relief until healing is complete.

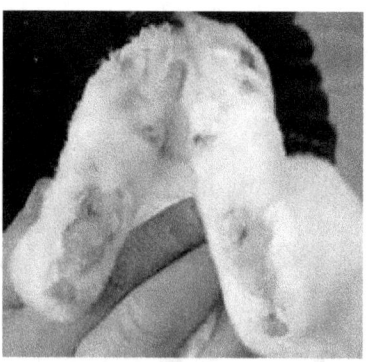

Sore hocks on a New Zealand White

Reproductive Problems and Genital Diseases

Caked Udder

Symptoms: Does that are heavy milk producers are the most commonly affected, particularly when nursing only a few young. The teats become sore, and the udder inflamed. The udder is hard and hot to the touch. The doe may refuse to nurse the litter due to pain.

Cause: The most common cause is too few young to relieve the flow of milk. Also, a doe will easily bruise herself when leaping in or out of the litter box if the sides of the box are too high. Or improper weaning.

Treatment: For mild cases such as improper weaning where the young were removed suddenly before milk production slowed, cut back on feed and return one or two of the litter for a day or two. Where too few young are being nursed, add one or more young from a doe with a large litter.

Where the teats are injured, sore or cracked, apply an antibiotic ointment which will not only aid in healing, but will soften the skin to prevent further cracking. This is frequently seen in does with their first litters.

Do not fail to treat a caked udder as soon as detected. If untreated it can lead to the destruction of the udder leaving it non-functional.

Cannibalism

Symptoms: Scattered bits of flesh or missing young from the nest box within two weeks after kindling.

Cause: Does with first litters are easily excitable and are under stress. They may eat their young if disturbed suddenly such as by a strange dog. However, it has been the author's experience that cannibalism will present itself when no disturbance has occurred. There seems to be two factors involved. The first is diet and the second is heredity. It may also be a method in which the doe reduces the number of young to what she can satisfactorily nurse.

Treatment: First decide the cause. If the doe was frightened and she became cannibalistic, prevent any further disturbance. Also, be careful to avoid unusual happenings or move her cage to a secluded spot before the arrival of future litters.

If diet is the cause, a protein supplement added to the ration a few days before kindling will provide a protein boost and aid in the production of milk. Where litters are large, moving some of the young to a doe having a small litter may save them. This is discussed earlier in Kindling and Care of the Young.

Mastitis

Symptoms: Tender, sore, or swollen milk glands with a bluish coloring. Severe cases may be abscessed.

Cause: An injury to the milk glands. The doe may have bruised herself when jumping into the nest box, or damaged herself on sharp objects such as nails, wires, or rough edges of the nest box. This is also caused by a bacterial infection entering the system, and young from an infected doe should not be placed in the nest box of an unaffected doe.

Treatment: Sanitize the nest box and hutch after each litter. Remove any sharp object within the hutch and ensure that each nest box has one side considerably lower than the other three sides. Treat with penicillin by injection continuing for 2 days after symptoms have disappeared.

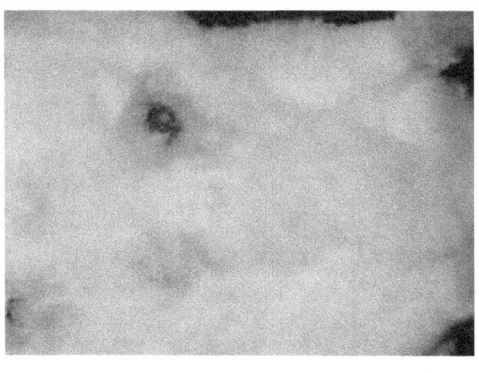

Doe With Mastitis

Orchitis
Symptoms: Inflammation of the testicles.

Cause: Bacteria which is transmitted from one rabbit to another during mating. Unclean cages and hutch floors.

Treatment: It is best to cull the affected buck from the herd rather than attempt treatment with antibiotics.

Vent Disease

Symptoms: The appearance of blisters or scabs on the genitals. Swollen genitals.

Cause: Vent disease is highly contagious and is frequently referred to among rabbit breeders as rabbit syphilis. If left untreated the rabbit will become a dormant carrier of the disease without any outward symptoms; it can then be transmitted to unborn young. The disease is caused by a bacteria.

It is possible to confuse vent disease with fungal or urine infection caused by unsanitary bedding. For proper diagnosis consult your veterinarian and have laboratory tests run.

Treatment: Wash the genital area with warm water and a mild soap. Apply an antibiotic ointment daily until the condition improves. Where solid floors are used, the straw or other litter material should be changed daily.

An injection of penicillin may be given deep in to the rear leg muscle. Consult the package insert for dosage and continue injections for 2 days after the disappearance of the symptoms.

Diseases Of The Eye And Ear

Conjunctivitis
Symptoms: This is an inflammation of the eye, and shows itself with tearing or a discharge of pus. In severe cases the eye may be stuck closed.

Causes: Bacteria which has infected the eye, or irritants such as dust, pollen or foreign objects.

Treatment: Cleanse the eye with a mild solution of boric acid, or sterile water. Apply an antibiotic ointment once or twice a day until the condition clears.

Ear Canker
Symptoms: Shaking the head and scratching at the ear. The formation of crust deep within the ear.

Cause: Ear mites which have embed into the soft parts of the ear.

Treatment: the mites which cause ear canker will spread quickly within the herd. Isolate affected animals. Apply a drop or two of baby oil to suffocate the offending mites, and repeat the treatment in 10 to 14 days. There are effective ear mite remedies available that contain insecticides and fungistats. Check with your local vet supply store.

Hereditary Conditions

Malocclusion or Buck Teeth
Symptoms: Loss of weight. Possible drooling and wetness about the mouth. Lower teeth that curve upward into the mouth, and upper teeth that curve inward into the mouth.

Cause: This is a hereditary condition where the upper and lower jaw is too long or too short. Rabbits must be able to gnaw on objects to keep the teeth worn down. When the teeth do not meet properly the proper gnawing action is lacking to wear them down and the teeth continue to grow. Death will result unless treatment is available.

Treatment: Using a pair of sharp wire nippers, temporary relief can be given by clipping the incisors. This will allow the rabbit to eat, but since the condition is hereditary the animal should not be used for breeding. With proper selection of breeding stock this condition is easily eliminated in future generations.

Splay Leg
Symptoms: Young rabbits with difficulty in standing. The legs spread away from the body and the animals sprawls on its belly. The very young rabbit will move about satisfactorily, but as it grows and gains weight moving about becomes more difficult. Once weaning occurs so that the doe does not enter the nest box to nurse the litter, splay leg causes the growing youngster

to find difficulty in reaching the feed. It soon gives up and dies.

Cause: This is another hereditary condition that can be eliminated through careful selection of breeding stock. The bones and muscles of the young never develop strength and there may even be some malformation of the hip joint.

Treatment: Dispose of young rabbits that show signs of having splay leg.

Young rabbit with congenital splay leg.

Parasites

Coccidiosis

Symptoms: A listless appearance, potbelly, loss of appetite, thinness and diarrhea. Upon examination the liver will be spotted white and the intestines inflamed. A heavy mucous will be found in the intestines.

Cause: Coccidia is a microscopic parasite that grow in the intestine. It is transmitted by drinking contaminated water or by the normal eating of offal.

Treatment: The use of sulfa solutions such as Sulmet on a regular monthly basis is a control measure. For acute cases use the solution for 3 days, then off 3 days, then give for a final 3 days. Follow instructions printed on the label as given for poultry.

Skin Mange

Symptoms: Intense itching, red, scaly skin, loss of hair. A crust of yellow, dried blood serum may be present.

Cause: A microscopic mite that burrows under the skin.

Treatment: Dust with a powder especially for external parasites such as fleas. Use two dustings, one week apart.

Tapeworm Larvae

Symptoms: There are no symptoms of tapeworm larvae in the live rabbit. Examination of the liver tissue will disclose white streaks, or there may be small, white cysts attached to the membranes of the stomach or intestines.

Treatment: No treatment is available. Prevention is the method of control as it is brought into the rabbitry by dogs and cats with the parasite. Fleas are the cause of transmission. Stray animals should not have access to the feed, water or nest material.

Warbles

Symptoms: Irritated, raised areas under the skin usually on the back, neck or flanks. Movement can be felt under the skin. A visible hole.

Cause: This is the larval stage of a bot fly which has entered under the skin and feeds upon tissue. It obtains oxygen through the hole in the skin and must frequently surface to breath. Newly hatched larva of the botfly penetrate the skin of the host animal that includes rabbits rodents and cats. Sometimes the female botfly lays eggs directly on the animals. The grub can also get into the animal through an open wound, the mouth or nose and then migrate inside the body of the host animal to a place under the skin. The larva makes a breathing hole and after a month it falls out having pushed its way out of the animal. There can be several in one location. The most common areas inside the animal are: along jawbone, around face, under belly and side. In the case of rabbits, the dewlap.

Treatment: A drop of chloroform or ether on the larvae will quiet it for easy removal with a pair of tweezers or forceps. The larvae may be as much as 1 ½ inches in length. After removal, apply a skin antiseptic to the wound.

The warble fly, or Bot fly, often called the stable fly, and larva.

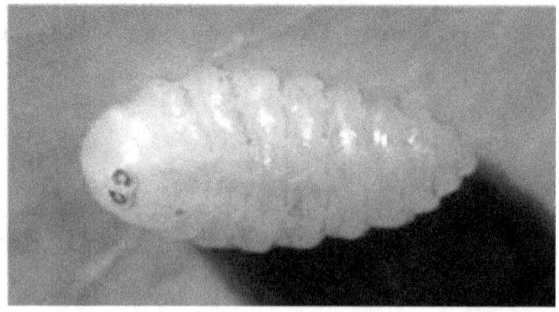

Stress Related Conditions

Ketosis

Symptoms: The rabbit refuses to eat, usually after kindling and following a normal pregnancy.

Cause: This is a metabolic disorder that releases ketone bodies into the blood stream. The presence of ketones prevents hunger and produces the normal action of the body to absorb body fat. This in turn causes weight loss and eventual death.

Treatment: A change of diet is effective. Changing from pellets to alfalfa hay and grain will stimulate an interest in food. Also, adding sugar or molasses to the drinking water will get the sugar into the blood stream rapidly and stop the manufacture of ketones. Does that are heavy milk producers are more generally affected by ketosis.

General Stress

Symptoms: All growing and breeding animals are under stress. Also, stress is seen in animals that are hauled to and from shows or otherwise moved from their normal quarters. Extremes of temperature, poor diet, parasites, illness, and strange visitors are other causes of stress. There may be diarrhea, unthriftiness, loss of weight, and in the case of pregnant does, aborted litters.

Cause: Any situation that puts a strain on the emotional or physical condition of the animal.

Treatment: Use a vitamin mixed with the water and feed a highly nutritional diet. Avoid drafty quarters or over-heated quarters that may cause bucks to go sterile. Treat disease and parasites as quickly as they become recognized.

Heat Prostration
Symptoms: Rapid breathing, prostration, and blood-tinged fluid emerging from the nostrils and mouth in severe cases.

Cause: Does that are due to kindle and overweight, older rabbits are most susceptible to extreme outside temperatures. Rabbits are heat sensitive animals.

Treatment: Reduce the temperature of surrounding air by spraying the area with water. Place wet blankets or frozen jugs of water inside the cages for the rabbits to lay on or against to reduce body temperature.

Slobbers
Symptoms: The rabbit will be wet about the face and throat, and the face may be swollen.

Cause: Slobbers is due more to management than to stress. It is caused by the feeding of fresh greens in excessive amounts when the digestive system is not accustomed to them. A sudden change in diet from pellets to greens is harsh on the animal's system and any change should be made gradually. An abscessed molar tooth may also be the cause.

Treatment: Discontinue the green feed until the condition clears itself. Do not give more greens than a rabbit will eat in 30 minutes time. Where an abscessed tooth is involved, it can be removed.

Transporting by wagon

Transporting

Whether you are set up as a large breeding operation or have a small family herd of rabbits there may be a time when traveling and transporting the rabbits is essential. You will want it to be safe and satisfactory with as little stress on the animals as possible. Rabbits can be transported easily if you take the proper precautions to care for them along the way. Since heat is the most hazardous condition facing the rabbit, it is imperative to provide as cool a transport as possible. Rabbits can only regulate their body temperatures by letting cool air pass over their ears; they do not perspire. Here is how to ensure a comfortable, safe trip for your rabbits by truck, car, jeep, plane or in a trailer.

Have on hand cages that are suitable for transporting. You can purchase them or make them yourself. Be sure they are of proper size for the breed that you are transporting. Make a way for securing the cage or cages so that they do not shift or tip during travel. Cages used for travel should be made of sturdy wire with a wire floor that fits into a watertight tray to catch urine.

Although wire floors aren't usually good for rabbits' feet, for occasional travel it's harmless and convenient. The tray hooks on so that the cage moves as a unit, similar to a birdcage with a removable bottom. Prefabricated cages come in many sizes and configurations based on the size of the rabbit and how many rabbits are to fit in the cage with separators. Never place two rabbits, especially two male rabbits, in the same section of a divided cage.

If you plan on traveling by plane, contact the airline about regulations for transporting animals and regulation cage sizes before obtaining or constructing your travel cages. Cages for an airline may be different than those you would use in your car, truck or van.

No matter what type of transportation you use, it is essential that the food dishes and water bowls are securely fastened so that they do not move around during the trip. It may be possible to get dishes and water bowls that screw to the cage walls. If transporting for 10 hours or less, no food or water is necessary for the journey unless the temperature is high, in which case water is essential. Upon arrival at the destination be sure to feed and water the animal. Since water is messy when traveling you should only put a little in the bottom of the water crock for the journey.

Before placing the rabbit in the cage for the trip, place a layer of absorbent material into the bottom tray. Use enough material to absorb any waste from the rabbit as well as spilled water. This could be cedar chips or straw, but dog pads are cleaner and neater for tray liners and are preferred by airlines. Place the cage into the tray and clip them securely together.

Once the rabbit is placed in the cage, secure the cage so that it will not shift or tip. If you are traveling far, a layer of foam under the cage can help to cushion the rabbit's ride. If you are traveling in an open pickup, cover the cage with a tarp to protect from wind and rain. This cover also offers security and less stress for the rabbit.

Once in transport, drive evenly without sudden acceleration or braking. Since animals can't anticipate motion, you should drive as though you have a blind guest in your vehicle to keep the animal as calm as possible. Make occasional stops to check on the animals. Rabbits prefer a dark, cool environment and are more sensitive to extreme heat than they are to extreme cold, so run the air-conditioner in your vehicle if it is a hot or warm day and you are traveling in a closed van or car.

By all means keep the sun off the rabbits. Automobile window shades or large sheets of cardboard work well. You can place these in the windows or directly over the cages, but don't block your view while driving. As mentioned earlier, a tarp works well to cover the cages. It also helps to make the rabbits feel more secure.

Keep the vehicle cool when you stop by parking in shaded areas. Leave the car running with the air conditioner on if necessary. If it is cool enough outdoors, leave the windows down sufficiently to keep the air circulating.

As soon as you arrive at your destination refill the food and water dishes. Then, let the rabbits get settled into the temporary environment, and don't take the rabbits from their cages unnecessarily. A good item to have on hand is a small watering can with a narrow spout like the ones used for houseplants to add water to the crocks. With a watering can, you can refill the water right through the wire cage without disturbing the rabbit.

Since the animals are stressed, don't handle them during travel. Too much handling will only increase stress for the rabbit and raise its body temperature.

How To Butcher And Skin A Rabbit

There are different ways of killing the domestic rabbit. A sharp blow to the base of the head, done correctly, results in instant death. The blow by itself dislocates the neck resulting in death. This is one of the oldest methods and once was very common. Although this method is efficient in itself, there is room for error, especially if the person doing the killing is squeamish or inexperienced. Experience brings proficiency.

Karate Chop Method

1. Hold the rabbit by the hind feet, head down. He may struggle at this unusual position, but will settle down and relax. You can also hold a smaller fryer rabbit at the loin.

2. His back, should be straight up and down, and will form a V with the ears, which will be alertly forward. You want a generous V. If the ears are not forward, move them a bit more forward.

3. While holding the back legs firmly, strike the rabbit a sharp blow to the point of the V - immediately behind the ears. Strike downward as to miss the shoulders.

4. If you're strong, you can deliver a karate-chop with the edge of your hand. If unsure of the power in your hand, use a pipe approximately 30-inches long.

5. Immediately hang the rabbit by the hind legs, even while in the throes, on heavy hooks, or with slip knots in shoelaces secured by a nail in the side of the butchering space.

6. Immediately cut the head off. Cut along the same line as the blow you struck. Your knife will slip easily through the dislocation in the neck

7. Allow the rabbit to finish bleeding dry.

Another method of killing is called the arterial bleed, and this is the method that the author uses. It is also the method stated in the Bible to be humane.

Arterial Bleed

1. Some people place the rabbit on the ground in front of a handful of alfalfa or other treat. The author simply hangs the rabbit by its hind legs with a rope or twine attached to a clothesline spanning between two posts specifically for butchering, then cuts through the jugular. In less than a minute, the rabbit is dead.

2. Once it bleeds out, you can remove the head. If you have trouble cutting through a joint in the neck bones, you can dislocate the neck with the same motion utilized in the above method, and then cut off the head.

The Broomstick Method

1. Place the rabbit's head on the ground and use a broomstick or other straight pole to lay across the rabbit's neck.

2. Step on one side of the broomstick.

3. Quickly step on the other side of the broomstick, and then pull the rabbit's body upward by the hind legs. Pull firmly until you feel the neck bones give. This will feel like a give and a stretch.

4. Cut off the rabbit's head through the break in the neck. This involves cutting through muscle and fur only, since the neck bones are completely separated.

5. Hang the rabbit by the hind legs to complete the rabbit cleaning.

Skinning

Step 1: Break the skin

While the rabbit is still hanging on the clothesline or other place where you have hung it, gather the skin around an ankle, pulling it tight so you can make an incision completely around the anklebone.

Step 2: Taking the skin off

Pull the skin down off the leg. Repeat the process on the other leg. Now work from the rabbit's hips to its head, pulling the skin inside out as if removing a jacket or coat.

Step 3: Remove extremities

Use game shears or a heavy knife to remove the rabbit's feet and head if it wasn't removed already.

Step 4: Take the guts out

Make a straight cut through the rabbit's belly from the rib cage to the pelvis. Open the sides of the belly and grasp the windpipe below the severed neck and pull it out.

Step 5: Cutting the meat

Remove the front legs by cutting under the shoulder blades. Remove the back legs by cutting through the hip sockets. For the tenderloins, cut the belly flaps away on both sides. Next, cut through the spine in two places; below the rib cage and above the hips on the other end.

A fryer is a rabbit between 1 and 3 pounds that's less than 12 weeks old. Fryers are fine grained and a bright pink color; they may be cooked the same as chicken. They are tender and tasty.

A roaster can be any size and must be over 8 months old. Roasters are coarse grained and the meat is a little darker than a fryer. Roasters can be tough, so they are usually stewed or braised.

Rabbit can be canned like any other meat and stored on the pantry shelves in jars with sealed lids, or it can be frozen. Rabbit jerky is made from the thin belly meat when butchering several rabbits and there is plenty of this thin meat, or it can be made from thin slices cut from other parts. Season each strip with salt, or add a very small amount of liquid smoke to soy sauce and brush it on the meat, then run a toothpick through one end, and hang it from a rack in the oven. Dry the meat at a low temperature such as 170 degrees F. or lower with the door ajar to allow moisture to escape. You can also use a dehydrator.

A skinned rabbit cut into portions for cooking.

How To Can Rabbit Meat

Occasionally you will find very old pressure canners for sale at yard sales or thrift stores. Models made before the 1970's were heavy-walled kettles with clamp-on or turn-on lids. They were fitted with a dial gauge, a vent pipe in the form of a petcock or covered with a counterweight, and a safety fuse. These can still be used satisfactorily, but pressure canners for use in the home were extensively redesigned beginning in the 1970's, and they are easier and safer to use. Most modern pressure canners are lightweight, thin-walled kettles; and have turn-on lids fitted with gaskets. There is at least one style still made with heavy cast aluminum, has screw-down knobs around the canner and does not have a gasket, however.

Modern pressure canners have removable racks, an automatic vent/cover lock, a vent pipe (steam vent), and a safety fuse. Use only canners that have the Underwriter's Laboratory (UL) approval to ensure their safety.

Today's pressure canner may have a *dial gauge* for indicating the pressure or a *weighted gauge*, for indicating and regulating the pressure. *Weighted gauges* are usually designed to "jiggle" several times a minute or to keep rocking gently when they are maintaining the correct pressure. Read your manufacturer's directions to know how a particular weighted gauge should rock or jiggle to indicate that the proper pressure is reached and then maintained during processing. *Dial gauge* canners will usually have a counterweight or pressure regulator for sealing off the open vent pipe to pressurize the canner. This weight should not be confused with a weighted gauge and will not jiggle or rock as described for a weighted gauge canner. Pressure readings on a dial gauge canner are only registered on the dial and only the dial should be used as an indication of the pressure in the canner. One manufacturer also makes a *dual-gauge* canner; read the manufacturer's user manual for information on when and how to use either the weighted gauge or the dial.

Pressure canners come deep enough for one layer of quart or smaller size jars, or deep enough for two layers of pint or smaller size jars. The USDA recommends that a canner be large enough to hold at least 4 quart jars to be considered a pressure canner for the USDA published processes.

Serious errors in processing can occur if any of the following conditions exist:

- The altitude at which the canner is operated is above sea level and adjustments in pressure are not made. Internal canner pressures (and therefore temperatures) are lower at higher altitudes. Canners must be operated at increased pressures as the altitude increases. Check reliable canning instructions for altitude adjustments.

- Air is trapped in the closed canner during the process. Air trapped in a pressure canner lowers the temperature obtained for a given pressure (for example, 10 or 15 pounds pressure) and results in under-processing. To be safe, USDA recommends that all pressure canners must be vented 10 minutes before they are pressurized.

-

  To vent the canner, lock the canner lid in place. Heat the canner on high until the water boils and generates steam that can be seen escaping through the open vent pipe or petcock. When a visible funnel-shape of steam is continuously escaping the canner, set a timer for 10 minutes. After 10 minutes of continuous steam, you can close the petcock or place the counterweight or weighted gauge over the vent pipe to begin pressurizing the canner.

- An inaccurate dial gauge is used. Dial gauges should be checked for accuracy each year before use. If the gauge reads high or low by more than two pounds at 5, 10 or 15 pounds pressure, replace it. If it is less than two pounds off in accuracy, you can make adjustments needed to be sure you have the required pressure in your canner.

Pressure canner showing both the dial
gauge and pressure regulator in place.

Procedure for canning rabbit: Choose freshly killed
and dressed, healthy animals. Dressed chicken or rabbit
should be chilled for 6 to 12 hours before canning.
Dressed rabbits should be soaked 1 hour in water
containing 1 tablespoon of salt per quart, and then
rinsed. Remove excess fat. Cut the chicken or rabbit into
suitable sizes for canning. Can with or without the
bones.

Hot pack – Boil, steam or bake meat until about two-thirds done. Add 1teaspoon salt per quart to the jar, if desired. Fill jars with pieces and hot broth, leaving 1-1/4 inch headspace.

Raw pack – Add 1 teaspoon salt per quart, if desired. Fill jars loosely with raw meat pieces, leaving 1-1/4 inch headspace. Do not add liquid.

Adjust lids and process following the recommendations according to the canning method used, which is using a dial-gauge or weighted gauge.

Table 1. Recommended process time for Chicken or Rabbit in a dial-gauge pressure canner.

Style of Pack	Jar Size	Process Time	Canner Pressure (PSI) at Altitudes of			
			0-2,000 ft	2,001-4,000 ft	4,001-6,000 ft	6,001-8,000 ft
Without Bones:						
Hot and Raw	Pints	75 min	**11 lb**	12 lb	13 lb	14 lb
	Quarts	90	**11**	12	13	14
With Bones:						
Hot and Raw	Pints	65 min	**11 lb**	12 lb	13 lb	14 lb
	Quarts	75	**11**	12	13	14

Table 2. Recommended process time for Chicken or Rabbit in a weighted-gauge pressure canner.

Style of Pack	Jar Size	Process Time	Canner pressure (PSI) at Altitudes of	
			0 - 1,000 ft	Above 1,000 ft
Without Bones:				
Hot and Raw	Pints	75 min	**10 lb**	15 lb
	Quarts	90	**10**	15
With Bones:				
Hot and Raw	Pints	65 min	**10 lb**	15 lb
	Quarts	75	**10**	15

This section was adapted from the "Complete Guide to Home Canning," Agriculture Information Bulletin No. 539, USDA, revised 2009.

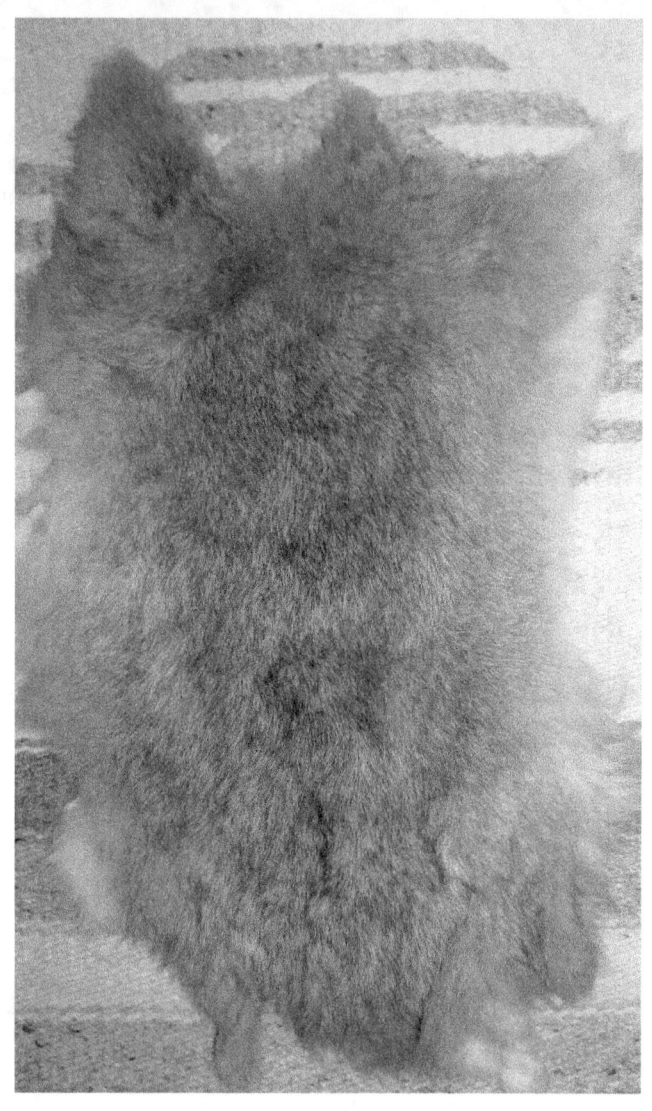

The Art Of Tanning Skins

Probably the most valuable by-product of the rabbit is the pelt. This luxurious fur can be used in a multitude of ways and is sought after by companies manufacturing everything from clothing to novelties. Many fur buyers purchase rabbit skins, and rabbit growers have found a good income from selling the pelts. But if you want the satisfaction of tanning your own hides and you take pride in producing something made by hand, then you will enjoy the challenge of tanning. There are two methods of doing so, one is to leave the fur on the hide, and the other is to remove it.

When the author first began tanning, she wanted to make bed covers. However, the weight of many tanned hides sewn together to cover a bed was much too heavy unless one sleeps in an igloo. The hide is better suited for the making of leather objects such as purses, sofa throws, car seat covers, small rugs, hatbands, and knife sheaths. After tanning, the pelts are cut and fit together then stitched. The scraps can be used for small items or for trim.

The author's preferred method is to leave the fur on because if you raise multi-colored rabbits you get a variety of color in the finished product, and solid white pelts can be dyed to achieve almost any color scheme you want to create. The fur is so lovely it is a shame to remove it.

The recipe contained here will tan six rabbit hides or eight squirrel hides. It is also sufficient to do one goat or deer hide. To do larger animals such as a steer you will need to increase the amount by doubling or tripling the ingredients and also to lengthen the processing time for each step. Don't fool yourself into thinking that just because the tanning process is a simple one that it does not involve work. The real work begins once the hides are tanned and you begin working them to make them soft and supple. This softening process is tedious but it must be done to get a soft and supple skin.

Where length of time to leave the skin in the solution is given, time is not so critical that you can not leave it a day or two longer if you have something else come up. Lightweight skins such as squirrel requires less time than do heavy skins such as steer. It is best to practice on small lightweight skins until you feel comfortable before attempting a large heavy skin. Because so many factors affect the tanning process the time limits are not necessarily exact.

Skins vary in thickness and weight and the ingredients may work slower or faster not only due to the thickness of the skin, but also according to the temperature of the air. It is essential that you check your hides frequently for predicted results. When the skin has reached the desired point the purpose has been achieved and you may go to the next step.

Even though you can do tanning anywhere it is best to set aside a certain work area that will not be disturbed.

The basement, garage, shop, or back room of your home will all make satisfactory work areas. I use a spare bedroom, as the space required is no more than space needed for a large pickle crock. Although the temperature is not critical, normal room temperature is ideal for all phases.

Most of the tools required for tanning are already in your home. Because the chemicals you will be working with are hard on the hands, wear protective rubber gloves and a plastic or rubber apron. When pouring the acid, be sure not to splash it on your skin or clothing. Always pour the acid into the water; never pour water into the acid. You cannot be too careful when working with acid, and above all, keep it out of the reach of children.

To start, you will need three large polyethylene garbage cans or similar containers. Begin by obtaining the necessary ingredients. Most of the ingredients are available from drug stores, but some may have to be purchased through mail-order suppliers or on the Internet.

Step One: Preparing The Skin

The foundation of the whole tanning process is preparing the skin. You cannot do a good job of tanning unless the skin is properly prepared. When you skin an animal you typically leave flesh on the skin. Before it can be tanned, all of the flesh must be removed, as well as the slippery membrane between the flesh and the skin, which enables the skin to move around while on the animal. This is done by spreading the skin out, hair side down, on a flat surface such as a table or counter

top that you won't be using for other things for several days.
Cover the skin well all over with salt, being careful not to leave any minute spot where there is no salt. Allow this to cure for a few days. Three or four days is good; if left longer the skin begins to dry out and is difficult to work with.

After the curing time, shake off all the salt and sit down with a good, sharp knife. Now scrape off the meat scraps and membrane from the skin. Do not cut holes in the skin, although it is all right to remove some of the skin beneath the membrane as a thin skin makes softer leather. Take your time with this step as it will take a while. Be careful to remove all traces of fat and flesh, getting down into the skin.

When you are satisfied with the results, wash the skin to remove all traces of salt, fat and scraps of meat. This washing will help keep your tanning solution clean so that it can be reused.

Step Two: Break Up The Glue

All skins contain glue, and this must be removed or you will end up with a stiff hide. To make the solution to break up the glue you will need commercial *Sulfuric Acid* from the drugstore. Handle the acid with caution and keep it in a safe place. Wear rubber gloves and a rubber or plastic apron.

Put five gallons of water into one of the containers then gently pour five liquid ounces of acid into the water. Use a plastic or a glass measuring cup. Add three pounds of salt, and stir very gently until the salt is dissolved. A mop handle, large dowel or yardstick may be used. Next immerse the skin into the solution; stir it to be sure there is no air bubble preventing the acid solution from reaching every part. Allow the skin to remain in the acid bath for four days, stirring several times a day to get the glue broken evenly.

On the fourth day, cut off a small piece of the skin and look at the cut edge. It should be white all the way through. If it is not white, if it still has a dark line in the middle, place the skin back in the solution and let it remain until an area of the thickest part becomes white all the way through.

Step Three: Neutralizing

When the skin has passed the whiteness test it is time to neutralize the acid to stop its action. Continued action on the skin will weaken it. Wearing your gloves, remove the skin from the solution with the mop handle and place it under running water. Depending on the size of the skin you can run water in the sink or in the bathtub for this. Rinse it thoroughly. Fill a second container with five gallons of water. Add one-third pound of baking soda and two pounds of salt. Stir this solution well and add the skin. It will probably foam. Leave the skin in this neutralizing solution for several days, stirring it several times a day.

On the second day, add another one-third pound of baking soda and stir. Repeat again on the third day making sure to stir each time. At the end of the third day the acid should be neutralized and skin soft.

Step Four: Removing The Hair

The hair can be removed at this point. If not wanting to remove the hair, skip this step and go on to the next. Remove the skin from the neutralizing solution and rinse it well in clear water. Squeeze out all the excess water so the skin is damp.

Put five gallons of clear water in a container and add three quarts of *builders' lime*. This can be procured from a lumber or building supply company. Stir the solution to dissolve the lime then add the skin, stirring it as before to releases any air bubbles and to allow the solution to reach every part of the skin. Stir twice daily. Do this every day until the hair comes out easily.

Now remove the skin from the solution and scrape the hair way. After removing the hair, wash the skin several times in a detergent and water solution. Wash it, wring it out and wash it again. Follow the washing by rinsing it several times in clear water to remove all traces of detergent.

Step Five: Tanning

Now begins the actual tanning process. From a drugstore or feed store buy two pounds of *alum*, or *aluminum sulfate*. Put five gallons of water in a container; add one and one-half pounds of salt and two pounds of alum. Stir to dissolve the salt and the alum, and then place the skin into this solution. The skin must remain in this solution for 12 days or so. Stir it gently once a day. The container should be covered.

After 12 days (or longer if necessary) the skin will be tanned and may be a light green in color. An evenly tanned skin will be evenly colored throughout the entire skin.

Step Six: Softening

Remove the skin from the tanning solution and rinse it in clear water. Spread it out and stretch it so the air can reach both sides and allow it to damp dry. Do not let it dry completely.

To stretch the skin a frame may be used similar to a quilting frame. I tack my skins to boards and turn them every day to allow both sides to reach the air. After the skin has become damp-dry, take it down and begin to work it. This is the most difficult part of tanning. Pull the skin, stretch it and scrape it with a dull object such as a dull knife or rock. The next day stretch it again and add a little Neatsfoot oil to both sides. Use only a small amount; do not get the skin greasy. Work the oil into the skin to help soften it.

As you scrape and stretch, take up the slack with the tacks in the frame. Each time you take up the slack, scrape the skin again half an hour later. Do not allow the skin to dry in direct sunlight or it will dry too quickly. Until the skin is completely dry, take it down and work it often; you cannot work it too much. The skin should soften as it dries. When the skin is completely dry it is ready to make articles from. You may want to display it as a wall hanging or table cover.

Don't let the length of time involved discourage you. There is no reason why you cannot tan a nice hide the first try, and you will get better as you do more and more skins. Each succeeding tanning session will give you softer, more professional skins.

Early Bark Tanning

There were several methods of tanning skins in times past, such as alum tanning, rubbing the brains of the animal into the skin, and bark tanning. The method described here is for bark tanning and was probably the most widely used during the early settlement of this country. Typical trees used for bark tanning were any of the oaks, fir, certain willows, chestnut, sumac leaves, oak galls, canaigre root which is a plant widely found in western United States, birch, alder, hemlock. The leaves of bearberry, heather, bloodroot, alfalfa, tea, sweet gale, pomegranate rinds, certain fern rhizomes and wood-hops have also been used. In today's commercial operations 80-percent of bark tanning is done with high concentrated extracts of chestnut, mimosa, and quebarcho found in South America,

Preparation began in the spring when bark was gathered from felled trees. At that time of year the sap is rising and the leaves are just appearing, and the bark is easily peeled. After stripping the bark from the trees it was stored until winter when the tanning was usually done. However, the bark could be used either fresh or dried so long as it was gathered after the sap rose. In storing bark, it had to be kept dry as rain would leach out the tannin, leaving it less effective.

The hides would be obtained during a hunting outing, or in the case of farming in later years domestic animals were raised for butchering. If the hides had been dried, it was necessary to soak them in water to soften them. Fresh skins needed no soaking as they were already soft and pliable and ready for fleshing. The act of fleshing is the removal of fat and the slippery membrane between the flesh and the skin, hair side down, and scraping with a knife or other sharp tool. Care was taken not to cut into the skin as this would weaken the leather. Every bit of flesh and fat had to be removed. It was a long tedious process, especially when large, heavy skins were being tanned such as bison, bear or elk. Since the winters were often severe and food had already been gathered and stored, there was plenty of time to sit around a fire and flesh out the skins and later to work at softening them.

After the skin was fleshed it was necessary to remove the hair. This was done by submerging the hides in a tanning trough with a mixture of hardwood ashes and water. The tanning trough was usually a split, hollowed out log, but it could be any container except a metal one. The ashes from campfires were saved and collected for this purpose.

The hides were left in this gooey mixture of ashes and water until the hair could be pulled away easily. The person doing the work would regularly check to see if his skins were ready to be tanned, and would turn and stir them so that the lye from the ashes could reach every part. When the hair pulled away easily, usually in two to five or more days, the skin was removed and the hair scraped away with a blunt instrument. At this point the hides were washed to prevent the lye from continuing to work and thereby weaken the skin or destroy the leather. They were washed and rewashed.

The actual tanning process was the next step. The bark gathered earlier was pounded to a pulp and placed in the tanning trough. Water was added to it. The hides were then submerged in this mixture, called bark tan, until they were colored all the way through. Again the person doing the work would check on his skins daily to see if the bark tan had done its job and to turn and stir the skins. This step took a very long time with the length of time depending a great deal on the temperature and the weather, and the strength of the bark tan. A small hide in a very strong bark tan might be ready in a couple of weeks. On the other hand, a very heavy hide in a weaker solution could take months to tan all the way through.

When it was decided that the skin was colored through, it was removed from the tanning trough and rinsed; then it was worked. This meant that it was stretched and pulled and scraped and sometimes lightly oiled until it dried to a supple and soft leather. This was another time consuming task, for the skin had to be worked long and hard, sometimes put away for awhile and then taken up again before it dried, to make a nice piece of leather. Only the finest, softest leathers were used for clothing. Less soft leathers were put to other uses but they were considered no less valuable because of the time it took to produce the item.

About The Author:

J. Darlene Campbell raised rabbits on the family farm in Oklahoma to sell commercially, along with ducks, chickens and goats. She canned 300 quarts of vegetables each year from her large garden. She writes about homesteading, gardening and preserving food for national publications. She currently lives in Mayer, Arizona with her husband.

Notes

Notes

Notes